"Drawing from the deep wells of theological education and her own experience of trauma and schizoaffective disorder, Erin Michael Grimm's *Emergent Grace* offers a refreshing stream of spiritual encouragement and thoughtful wisdom for anyone distressed by serious mental illness. This book is a source of hope for all those who suffer from such illnesses, including loved ones, caregivers, health professionals, clergy, and the Christian church as a whole. I am grateful to God for this book and its author."

—Douglas Strong, professor of Wesleyan Studies, Seattle Pacific University

"Erin Grimm is a brilliant young thinker with a passion for uniting faith and the diversity of human experience. She offers a wealth of perspective as both a follower of Jesus and as a student of human behavior. I'm a big fan of her faithful (and faith-full!) commitments to holistic theological development."

—Jay Akkerman, professor of pastoral theology, Northwest Nazarene University

"This book displays Erin Grimm's deep Christian faith, her fierce moral earnestness, her gentle and gentling love for people who suffer, her extraordinary honesty about her own experience of emotional challenges, and her journey toward wholeness. Grimm invites readers to face and share their own stories with confidence, greatly expanding the conversation about the relationship between faith and mental illness in many fruitful directions."

—Richard B. Steele, professor of moral and historical theology, Seattle Pacific University

"*Emergent Grace* offers us a story—a story shaped by, but not ultimately defined by, serious mental illness (SMI). Erin Grimm shares her story, shaped by her faith and the grace of God. While not a mental health professional, Grimm shares her journey of the deep and abiding relationship between SMI and faith, medicine and therapy. She offers hope for many facing similar challenges. We need more stories like Grimm's."

—BRAD D. STRAWN, CHIEF OF SPIRITUAL FORMATION AND INTEGRATION OF THEOLOGY AND PSYCHOLOGY, FULLER THEOLOGICAL SEMINARY

"In this volume, Erin Grimm shares from experience rooted in substantial study. *Emergent Grace* is not lightweight encouragement to 'feel better.' It is just the right mix of research, personal stories, and solid wisdom. I commend both the writer and the word to you, with a prayer that you will learn to live joyfully into your created design as you navigate its limits."

—CAROLYN MOORE, AUTHOR OF *WHEN WOMEN LEAD*

"As the Scriptures invite the church to rejoice with those who rejoice and join in the struggle with those who are struggling, this act of compassionate presence is not about having all the answers, but a loving solidarity refusing to allow persons to suffer in suffocating solitary anonymity. This book invites those who suffer to find hope and others to embrace those who struggle with loving hospitality. Read and be challenged and encouraged."

—BRENT PETERSON, DEAN OF THE COLLEGE OF THEOLOGY AND CHRISTIAN MINISTRY, NORTHWEST NAZARENE UNIVERSITY; CO-AUTHOR OF *BACK SIDE OF THE CROSS*

"This is a book that is full of beautiful hope and severe mercies. Deep, muffled, but secure glints of light reach out through this text and by the spirit of Erin Grimm's profound knowledge. This is a book, a prayer, really, for those who need a whisper in their ear that you are beloved, you are worthy of love. Come and receive this sip of grace that says you can make it through this minute, this hour, this day, this year."

—JIM WELLMAN, CHAIR OF THE DEPARTMENT OF RELIGION, UNIVERSITY OF WASHINGTON

Emergent Grace

Emergent Grace

Christian Hope for Serious Mental Illness

ERIN GRIMM

Foreword by Lindsay Vernor

RESOURCE *Publications* • Eugene, Oregon

EMERGENT GRACE
Christian Hope for Serious Mental Illness

Resource Publications
An Imprint of Wipf and Stock Publishers
199 W. 8th Ave., Suite 3
Eugene, OR 97401

www.wipfandstock.com

PAPERBACK ISBN: 978-1-6667-6596-0
HARDCOVER ISBN: 978-1-6667-6597-7
EBOOK ISBN: 978-1-6667-6598-4

02/16/23

Disclaimer:
The information available in this book is presented in summary form as a
supplement to, and *not* a substitute for the knowledge, skill, and judgment of
qualified psychiatrists, psychologists, physicians, and health care professionals. Or clergy. The information has been obtained from sources believed to
be accurate and reliable. Information accessed on and through this book is
provided "as is" and without warranty, express or implied, including, but not
limited to, any implied warranty of merchantability or of fitness for a particular purpose. However, I make no warranty as to the accuracy, reliability
or completeness of this information. Should you have any health, medical or
disability questions or concerns, please consult a physician or other health
care professional. Information accessed on or through this book is neither
complete nor exhaustive and does not cover all disabilities, diseases, illnesses, and physical conditions or their management or treatment.

For Todd, in loving memory of Paul Lee, and with gratitude for the community at Seattle Pacific University, Seattle, WA

I'll make a covenant of peace with them that will hold everything together, an everlasting covenant. I'll make them secure and place my holy place of worship at the center of their lives forever. I'll live right there with them. I'll be their God! They'll be my people! The nations will realize that I, God, make Israel holy when my holy place of worship is established at the center of their lives forever.

—Ezekiel 37:26–28

Look at what I've done for you today: I've placed in front of you
Life and Good
Death and Evil.
And I command you today: Love God, your God. Walk in his ways. Keep his commandments, regulations, and rules so that you will live, really live, live exuberantly, blessed by God, your God, in the land you are about to enter and possess. But I warn you: If you have a change of heart, refuse to listen obediently, and willfully go off to serve and worship other gods, you will most certainly die. You won't last long in the land that you are crossing the Jordan to enter and possess. I call Heaven and Earth to witness against you today: I place before you Life and Death, Blessing and Curse. Choose life so that you and your children will live. And love God, your God, listening obediently to him, firmly embracing him. Oh yes, he is life itself, a long life settled on the soil that God, your God, promised to give your ancestors, Abraham, Isaac, and Jacob.

—Deuteronomy 30:15–20

Contents

Contents

Foreword

DEAR READER,

It is the season of Advent as I write these words to you, sitting on my couch instead of at my desk so that my two little dogs can curl up next to me. My candle that smells like a fir tree is burning, even as my heart burns in prayer for you, dear one.

Advent, which marks the beginning of the Christian calendar or "church year," is the month leading up to Christmas Day wherein we who are Christians pause in the darkness "before" the Light of the World is born. Oh, we know that the man, Jesus of Nazareth, was born long ago, but Advent (from the Latin *adventus*, which means "coming") is a time to anticipate the arrival of our coming Savior. We do this by situating ourselves in the traditional Christmas narratives of chapter 2 of the Gospel of Luke and chapters 1 and 2 of the Gospel of Matthew. But we also do this by acknowledging that we are living in a world that has not yet been restored by God.

It is a season where we wait expectantly—in hope—for the coming restoration. But this is not a passive waiting, nor is it a "wishful thinking" version of hope. It is a hope that is grounded in the certainty of God's love for us. It is a hope that believes, trusts, and acts as if someday God will make all things new, because God has promised to do so. In the one hand, we hold the darkness of our lived experience and the suffering we see in the world. In the other hand, we hold the promise of restoration, newness, and healing. During Advent, we acknowledge the tension between these two realities, and we choose to sit in it.

I am no mental health expert, nor have I been diagnosed with a serious mental illness (SMI), but I imagine that this tension is similar to what those who have experienced SMI contend with much of the time.

In this work, Erin demonstrates how she has wrestled with the tension of a false reality and reality as it was, with a mental illness diagnosis and a disordered perception of what it means to be a "good" Christian, with a misconstrued identity of self and a holistic understanding of self, and ultimately, with despair and hope that often exist side-by-side. By pairing treatment from mental health professionals with care for one's spiritual self through a holistic theological framework, Erin proffers a means for the healing of the whole self. Quick to reject any recommendation of refusing medicine as part of treatment, she suggests that, in attending to one's spiritual health, one can find health and wholeness even as one continues a treatment plan that includes medicine. She also advocates for holding space for a healing that no longer requires medicine.

The primary content of this book is bookended by theological voices who proclaim "the grace of limitations" and the dignity of choice aligned with God's heart for human flourishing. These voices center this conversation of mental illness and lived theology in the abundant love that God has for us as humans who were created in God's image. From this place of belovedness, Erin explores in chapter 2, the theological framework of the Wesleyan Quadrilateral (Scripture, tradition, reason, experience) as a balanced foundation for combatting the obscurity that SMI often perpetuates. In chapter 3, she takes a step back, looking at the big picture of how mental illness, social justice, and our lived theology impact and are impacted by society at large. She urges us to acknowledge our "situatedness" by remembering first that we are all made in the image of God, even as we reckon with our communal and individual particularities. Chapter 4 includes a deep dive into the despair and hope experienced by the nation of Israel, even as it surpasses its historical significance, metaphorically proclaiming the same hope for us today. The book ends as it began . . . in hope. But don't skip the Appendix! It is full of relatable snapshots from Erin's blog that resonate so deeply and on so many different levels. As a teaser, my two favorite entries are called "Snapping Out of It Is Bad" and "What the Schizophrenia Spectrum Teaches All of Us about Being Christian."

Erin and I met as fellow students through the online MDiv program at Northwest Nazarene University (NNU). In no time at all, I realized that her perspective was one that I needed. It continues to shape me. She has become a friend, an advocate, an encourager, and a voice of wisdom as I seek to live out my own calling. Her transparency inspires and invites me to keep becoming the best version of my own authentic self. It is a privilege and an honor to invite you to grab a warm cup of coffee, tea, or hot chocolate and curl up on your own couch to read the beautiful words of my beautiful friend.

Whether you are someone who has experienced SMI, someone walking alongside a friend or loved one with SMI, or simply someone who has to relate to other people regardless of SMI, this book will offer you profound insight into the human experience and into the soul. I encourage you to receive it as the gift that it is: a bridge between mental health and lived theology, a reminder that you are deeply loved, and a beacon of hope.

Rev. Lindsay Vernor
December 2022
Nampa, Idaho

Preface

IN 2015, AFTER FOUR years of increasing deterioration of my mental health, I was hospitalized, twice within a four-month period, with schizoaffective disorder. I was not informed that I had the disorder until three years later, in 2018, because the news of such a devastating diagnosis has led people to self-hatred to the extent of provoking suicide.

If this applies to you, don't give up, and read this book.

Schizoaffective disorder is a combination of schizophrenia and bipolar disorder, so I have lived experience of delusions without mania and, at a different time, full-blown mania (if I had had delusions only with mania, then it would be called bipolar disorder with psychotic features). Thus, I have personal experience of both schizophrenia and bipolar disorder, though with some variations due to my suffering from a combination of the two.

My illness also comes paired with chronic complex post-traumatic stress disorder (C-PTSD), though in this book I will not focus on my trauma or how I acquired it. In many ways this book isn't even about me. It's about *us*, people who need medicine, and who experience severe mental health challenges. Particularly helpful has been my ability to approach my mental health challenges with a growth mindset. I have learned to see my crises as opportunity for change and personal development. I now welcome challenges—I still encounter them—as an opportunity to partner with my family and to mature in my Christian walk, which has enriched my ability to hold space for others with (more) compassion and grace. I'm not perfect—who is?—but my high standards for my behavior come from my Christian calling, and my medicine and self-care make living well possible on most days.

What do health and mature cultivation of my mind look like?

I make sure I get out in nature, exercise daily, eat healthy food, and I am intentional as I tend to my physical, mental, emotional, relational, marital, and professional health on a daily basis. These are research-based practices for living with serious health challenges, and they also bring me joy (when I'm having a hard time, I give myself permission to take a break).

One thing that does *not* bring me joy is reading the news or watching it on television. The news feeds anxiety, and it covers serious mental illness (SMI) in a very negative way. With its coverage of shootings, the news can give people who are really struggling bad ideas, or provoke shame even in people who aren't struggling with dark and shameful thoughts.

Also, social media can contribute to obsession with "likes" and "hearts" and "shares." It contributes to eating disorders and persistent insecurity, especially in young women. I am rarely on social media.

I recommend you read this book slowly but all the way through, returning to it again and again until it becomes second nature to think about your health with hope and without stigma, but with realism that doesn't deny the reality of SMI. Also, don't think you need to share about your condition with anyone. I am called to share and so am very open, but there is still a lot of discrimination out there, so share carefully and when you're ready to allow people to have their own response, without controlling the outcome of how it may or may not change a relationship.

This book teaches the Wesleyan way, but I don't think that you need to be in a Wesleyan denomination (for example, a Nazarene, a Methodist, or a Pentecostal) to be a Wesleyan. Wesleyanism is about the *via media*—the middle way—and it is the fruit of its founder's intensive study of the Gospels and the full canon of Scripture, and the early church. John Wesley (1703–91) was a practical theologian. He was also deeply ecumenical, meaning that he was not obsessed with a specific denomination (he was committed to the Anglican Church). I respect all forms of Christianity if they work for the person, but am particularly committed to seeing the church become more willing to extend *consistent* hospitality to those most marginalized, including those with SMI.

First self-published in 2020 on my website erinmichaelgrimm.com, *Emergent Grace* has been downloaded thousands of times. I have updated it now so that it will serve readers beyond the COVID-19 era and have found a publisher rather than self-publishing it, so that my writing will serve readers, with God's help, beyond the parameters of this time period. My thanks to Wipf and Stock Publishers and their Resources imprint for publishing this book.

My hope is that what follows is *helpful*, and that if it is not, *that you won't ever give up on yourself, or on your suffering loved one(s).* God loves you, God loves everyone, and no one is irredeemable. Hope makes all the difference. Always. Especially with health challenges, we must not lose hope. For several years I was a Buddhist Christian, though some Christians would say that that is an impossibility (and maybe they are right). Regardless, Buddhism helped me accept my suffering and to live at peace, but with becoming Christian again, I acquired *hope*.

That *hope* is unique to the Christian story and is what I want to share with you here. I believe Christian hope is the foundation of mental health recovery and maintenance. I believe this so strongly that I have spent the past seven years writing and then rewriting the book that you now hold in your hands. *Solo Deo gloria.* To God alone be the glory.

Erin Grimm
Sacramento, California
November 25, 2022

Acknowledgments

THANK YOU, BARBARA BROWN Taylor, for reviewing this work and for your encouragement as I wrapped up the writing process; thank you for your warmth and for focusing on the importance of hope. Your work is a lifeline to so many.

To my teachers, even the challenging and challenged ones: thank you for sharpening my character and sense of responsibility and accountability. To Dr. Doug Strong, for teaching me through his scholarship that you can merge vital piety and justice: thank you. To Dr. Brenda Salter McNeil, for teaching me to pursue real justice: thank you. To Dr. Peter Bellini, for devoting your career and scholarship to people like me: thank you.

Thank you to Matthew Wimer, managing editor at Wipf and Stock, for your cheer, and to George Callihan, editorial assistant, for handling numerous revisions with compassion and grace. Thank you, also, Caleb Shupe, format checker and copyeditor, for your valuable time. Thank you, Savanah N. Landerholm, for giving me a beautiful cover and for your careful typesetting. Special thanks also to Joe Delahanty in marketing and Emily Callihan in the editorial department.

To all faculty, staff, and administrators at Northwest Nazarene University, thank you for holding space for me and my dreams the last three years as I complete my MDiv in missional leadership online with you. Your sincerity and compassion as a faculty, especially that of Rev. Dr. Brent D. Peterson and Rev. Dr. Diane C. Leclerc, have been transformational. Thank you, Brent, for your healthy boundaries and unfailing warmth, charity, and grace. Thank you,

Diane, for trusting me with your students as I began to think about sharing this work in its present form and for teaching me the *via media*. Your book *Discovering Christian Holiness* is one of my absolute favorites. A special thanks to Dr. Jay Akkerman for his amazing prayers on my behalf. Thank you, also, for honoring women and our calls to ministry. So refreshing.

To my husband Todd, my wonderful family, including step-relations and in-laws: thank you for your sustaining and unfailing love. Thank you to my wonderful neighbors. Todd, you are the most important person in my life, my life companion, and soulmate. Not every husband supports his wife as she writes a book like this one.

Finally, to Dr. Richard B. Steele, you have meant the world. Thank you for the most authentic witness as a teacher I have ever experienced. This framework I have developed would not exist without you. Thank you for teaching me the Wesleyan way and, more important, for modeling it in your relationships with students.

This book touches on social justice quite a bit and I am privileged. All royalties for this book are established so that they are automatically routed to NNU (for an endowment for Latin American library materials) and SPU (towards an endowment for African-American seminarians) in gratitude for their vital, though imperfect, relationships with me, which have sustained me.

Introduction

MY APPROACH

I BRING A CHRISTIAN, integrative lens to the management of serious mental illness (SMI), by which I mean illnesses accompanied by psychosis. Psychosis can be a feature of depression, bipolar disorder, schizophrenia, and schizoaffective disorder, and perhaps other disorders, and is one of the reasons mental health challenges become chronic. This book addresses social ills as it tackles a more practical problem: therapists often aren't Christian, and those who are, are rarely trained in the Christian tradition as it might intersect with the practice of mental health care; and the Christian tradition, for better or worse, does not consistently integrate modern therapeutic and psychiatric models as it tends to the potentially very real, spiritual aspects of SMI.

Let me be clear from the beginning: I do not think that mental health challenges are a sign of damnation. I do, however, believe that they impact us spiritually, sometimes for the better (with the mystical) and sometimes for the worse (for example, hearing destructive voices that promote harmful or dangerous behaviors). By no means do I equate SMI to the demonic, though I do believe demonic spiritual forces can take advantage of challenging mental states, impacting us for the worse.[1] In my estimation, though I'm not ruling out

1. If you believe I am mistaken, this book is still for you. In addition to this book, merely look up reputable "deliverance" ministries. I personally have worked through spiritual blockages to the extent that I now view my mental

the possibility of exceptions, mental health challenges are similar to diabetes: as a diabetic requires insulin, I require medicine. Daily. In *Emergent Grace* I propose applying John Wesley's holistic and integrative approach to Christianity in the service of mental health recovery and maintenance. I am not writing as a professional minister, therapist, or psychiatrist, but rather as a current seminary student and a former ministry intern, hospice volunteer, and lay crisis counselor (a Stephen Minister), with lived experience of two mental health hospitalizations, one involuntary (2015).

Chapter 1 starts our time together with a word from clergy that responds to hardship pastorally and puts it in the larger framework of the Christian story.

Chapter 2 approaches management of SMI using the theological framework of John Wesley in hopes that it will help you find yours.

Chapter 3 is holistic. It touches on how society can contribute to negative mental health and general poor public health.

Chapter 4 shares true insights gained from my own valley of bones. It closes with my pastoral response to acute suffering and offers robust hope that is scriptural, based in a close reading of Ezekiel 37.

Chapter 5 I highly recommend if you're worried that you're damned or are worried that to go off your meds is a Christian thing to do. It also features a word from clergy on the topic.

The appendix is a central aspect of this work, do not skip it—it features my most popular blog posts, which were written at different times of my self-understanding as a person with SMI.

The afterword shares my thoughts on school and mental health, which is a major topic right now, and for so many reasons.

The Good Samaritan showed neighborly love to a person who was beaten and ritually unclean, while a priest walked by. To live out my commitment to the Christian faith, I defend the dignity of LGBTQIA+ folks, without letting that dictate my theological

---

health condition as a chemical imbalance.

or personal belief system. There will be no hate preached here, nor will there be partisan bickering advocating for one side over the other.

MY STORY, CONTEXT, AND AUDIENCE

When I think of all the drafts I have begun and left unfinished at the various times I have sat down to write this book, I am reminded of how many different ways I have viewed myself over the years as I have come to grips with the diagnosis of schizoaffective disorder. For the first two years of losing contact with reality, I did not have knowledge of what was happening to me except that everything had become remarkably difficult. There was the ebb and flow of experiencing extreme existential terror, followed by learning about what my suspicions were, reality testing them, and realizing I was safe. A moment of peace and calm would ensue once my deepest suspicions of betrayal or unpopularity were disconfirmed.

Upon having my paranoid thoughts disconfirmed, I would find life again to be effortless and wonderful, and I would reflect upon how difficult life must be for those who had indeed, for example, been falsely accused of being terrorists, or who had had other reasons to fear acutely for their very lives.

In a word, I suffered from delusions.

Now, in remission, in the safe fuzziness of an antipsychotic, an antidepressant,[2] and a mood stabilizer, I can let down my guard and write to you. I am white, and am in a relatively safe position to write this book, while many are not at liberty to reveal weaknesses because they already have enough persecution to deal with on a

---

2. Note: my involuntary hospitalization occurred when I was on a high dose of an antidepressant without a high dose of an antipsychotic. Antidepressants are crucial for me, but they come with an FDA black box warning because they can prove extremely dangerous when used without antipsychotics for SMI conditions. This is not medical advice. I am unqualified to give medical advice and am only sharing my personal experience. Discuss this in detail with your psychiatrist, doctor, and/or other qualified medical professionals.

daily basis. I have been able to find treatment and professionals. So many people in the United States, and in the larger world, lack these things. I went to a global mental health meeting held at the University of Washington in 2018. There, people discussed not a patient's right to refuse treatment, which is a common theme in the United States' debates around mental health; but rather, the broader right to obtain treatment in the first place, which is more of a need in the rest of the world (and among the uninsured in the United States). It is a question of access, and frankly, most people lack access.

As with every organization, there are problems with NAMI, but I won't insult the organization: the National Alliance on Mental Illness saved my life and they provide life-saving support to sufferers and their families and friends. My spouse, Todd, has said that he cannot imagine how differently things might have worked out if it weren't for NAMI, health insurance, and a woman we met along the way who knew how to combat the stigma of SMI with the power of storytelling. This woman's son has been in prison for several years with SMI of a severity that I have only touched briefly, and many years ago. But she was brave, and she shared her story so I could learn from it.

Jesus Christ our Savior is the best shaper of our stories, and if we contemplate his ways and commit to modified fellowship, insofar as our illnesses allow, then we can grow in a spirit of accountability and love, such as was modeled in the world-wide Wesleyan-holiness movement. We can find peace and accountability and rest in the knowledge of Christ, even amidst terrifying and alienating symptoms. My hope is to disciple my readers and encourage the growth of the Emergent Grace movement, comprised of Bible-believing Christians who embrace the good news and find hope in spite of their mental health challenges or the challenges of their loved ones.

1

The Grace of Limitations

MY KNOWLEDGE OF MYSELF and my treatment adherence, and my
ability to learn my limitations—in other words, my need to take
medicine indefinitely—and to stay within them, are what keep me
doing well to date. But none of this would have been possible without a sermon I heard on November 26, 2017. With my former pastor's permission, I am beginning my book with it. It sets the stage.
May it bring you some of the comfort and wisdom it has brought
me. Sermons have a way to speak to the heart, and they do this
with the training and authority that a lay person like myself just
can't beat. This sermon was written and preached by Rev. Dr. Chris
Pritchett, teaching elder, Presbyterian Church USA, in Seattle, WA.
The Scripture reading comes from Genesis 3:1–9. Title: "The Grace
of Limitations."

Most of us are aware that something is missing in our lives. It's true
for every human being on the planet, so you're not alone. But we
each have unfulfilled desires, unattained goals, things that we believe would make our lives better, happier, or more content if we
had them. In every garden of life, God has placed something that is
beyond our created reach. It is something we can see, but we cannot
have. For some it is a better past, and for others it's a desired future
that God has not created for you. It may involve work, health, a

relationship, or an achievement you desperately want, which may or may not be just beyond your reach.

But what if I told you we were designed this way? That the God we believe loves us with an unconditional love, who created us and brought us into being, also created us with this feeling that something is always missing in life? That the longing in each of our hearts and lives is meant to be there, and that finding joy and peace and contentment in life doesn't come from trying to satisfy our longing, but rather by embracing the longing and accepting life's limitations. That part of God's pathway to joy for us is that when we choose to live within our created limitations, we discover that we have everything we need, and life naturally becomes a gift of gratitude, rather than a problem to solve. Does life itself ever feel to you like the whole thing is a problem to solve, a destination for which we are all searching? This way of living comes with a perpetual low-grade angst. It is both exhausting and frustrating. But Genesis 3 helps us to see that we can be free from this inner struggle.

The first two chapters of the Bible are incredibly important because they reveal what God had in mind for us from the beginning. Before sin entered the world and before we started making our choices, God made clear what his choice was for us. And it was paradise. The rest of the Bible is essentially the drama of God's recovery plan after we started making our choices. But we can only imagine the beauty of the garden of Eden. The language of the text is not scientific or historic, but poetic and metaphorical. So, the garden was not so much an actual place as a relationship with God and all creation that was in the right place.

Humanity was blessed with the distinction of being made in the image of God. We were blessed to have good work caring for the garden God created. We were blessed with intimacy when God created partners for us, and we were blessed, as our text says today, with the freedom to eat of almost every fruit of the garden. We are still blessed with all of these created gifts. There is no question of that.

The question is, are we paying attention to our blessings? Blessings are not things we achieve for ourselves. They are gifts that come only from God's hands. And they account for the things we value most—someone to love, our unique talents, our health, the breath in our lungs, the rising sun every day. These are not things we earned. They come only by the hand of God. When we pay attention to our blessings, we soon realize that we cherish them so much more than our achievements. So all that is left is gratitude.

The verse of the poetry tells us little about the garden. Frankly, most of what we are told is focused on the limits of this paradise. The one thing described in considerable detail is the tree in the middle of the garden whose fruit Adam and Eve were forbidden to take.

The placement of this tree, in the midst of the garden, is incredibly significant. Had it been located on the distant fringe of the garden, they could have ignored it. But no, every day they had to walk by this tree that was not theirs for the taking. Remember this is before the fall. It's the garden God created and called good. So there is always something missing in paradise. That tree represents the object of your longing—the thing that is missing in your life.

I don't know what the tree symbolizes in your life. I know what it is in my life, and with some reflection you will remember what it is in yours. It isn't hard to find because, remember, it is in the middle of your garden. In some way, you pass by this tree every day.

Our text today finds Adam and Eve staring at the tree. They have to wonder what is so special about this fruit? Why can't they have it, too? Our theologians can tell us exactly what is special about the tree. It is the mark of God's grace upon their lives. This is the grace of limitations.

How can this be a grace when it feels like a curse?

It's a grace because it reminds them they are creatures and not creators. Only God creates life. In spite of all our hard work, we don't create our lives or really even "make a living." We receive life as God's unfolding drama. And this created mark of limitations is a grace because it means that God is set on dignifying humanity with the freedom to make choices. Without that limitation, there is no choice for humans. And no choice means no freedom, and no freedom means no dignity.

Every time you confront this thing that is missing from your life you have to decide how you will respond to it. It will either become the altar where you kneel in prayer before the God who alone is whole and complete, lacking in nothing, or it will drive you crazy as you obsess over how to find what you do not have. It's your choice. This is how God honors humanity like no other creature on earth.

Much of pop psychology today tries desperately to make you feel better by claiming that you are not to blame for your choices. But all that this really does is rob you of your created dignity. "You're a victim," some claim. "Blame your employer, your spouse, your environment," or best of all, "your parents." But that is not what our most primal poetry claims. Adam and Eve had a wonderful environment, and they had no parents to blame for their problems. Imagine that. Still, they chose to reach beyond their limitations. I'm not claiming we are not sometimes victimized, but we are still responsible for our own choices.

Never let anyone take away your created dignity to choose and to be responsible for your life.

The most fundamental, primal, choice we make is how we respond to created limits. In the words of theologian Karl Barth, all sin begins with ingratitude. Consider that idea for a moment: All sin begins with ingratitude. Even though God has created our garden and already called it "good," we take a hard look at what is missing and say it isn't good enough. Judging the work of the Creator in our lives to be too slow or too fast, too dull or too frightening, or simply too limiting, we reach for something more. We reach to become gods who can recreate life the way we want it.

We try to recreate not only our own lives, but also our spouses, children, employees, friends, anyone whom we deem not good enough. Who do we think we are? We are ungrateful. That's who we are. Gratitude always embraces limitations.

This is not to say that we should not try to make improvements in the garden of life. Of course we should diet, save, work hard, stand up for important causes, and strive to be all God created us to be. But there's a big difference between doing some gardening and becoming obsessed with a different garden. When we are grateful for the life we've been given, we look around and realize that even though something is missing, it's still a pretty incredible place to live. When we are not grateful, we ignore the thousands of fruitful trees we've been given and we pitch our tent under the one tree we cannot have. But when we reach for this one thing that's missing, it is then that we lose the garden. And on the way out of the gates we realize that it was paradise. Only now it is paradise lost.

A man flies in from out of town to bury his father who died suddenly. The son wanted so much to become somebody important in his career, so there wasn't time for a lot of visits home. On the plane ride to the funeral, the son decides to cope with his grief by writing a letter to his father. The letter essentially says, "I've always loved you, Dad." As the tears stream down his face, he curses himself for not writing sooner. What was this man's created limitation over which he reached? It was his career—he reached for too much—and it cost him grief and pain.

A woman sits in the first pew at her daughter's wedding. She's overwhelmed by how beautiful the bride is. Then she remembers all of the terrible arguments that drove them apart for so many years. She just wanted her daughter to be better, but now it all seems so meaningless. She wishes, desperately, that she could take back all of the harsh words she said. But as she watches her daughter take the hand of her groom, she knows those years are forever gone. Again, it is not until the garden is lost that we realize it was paradise.

According to our text, we had help in losing our good gardens. We were tempted by the serpent. But the Bible doesn't blame Adam and Eve's fall on the serpent. It blames Adam and Eve for choosing to believe his lie. Temptation is always a lie, and it's the exact lie we want to hear. The serpent tells us we can be like God and have it all. All we have to do is reach for more. But the only thing we really grab is regret.

As the sacred poetry continues, in the cool of the day God came looking for Adam and Eve. When he found them hiding, he killed one of his animals to cover their naked shame. And now, in Jesus Christ, has God come looking for you and me. He finds us busily sewing together fig leaves of excuses and blame. Then he sacrifices his life on the cross to cover our shame and restore our dignity. Why? Because God loves us too much to abandon us to our bad choices.

If human dignity begins by the grace of taking responsibility, which is what we call confession, it ends by accepting this even more amazing grace called forgiveness. I am amazed by how many people can make it through the first part and take responsibility for their actions, but they cannot accept grace as forgiveness. There is no dignity in simply claiming to be a sinner. It doesn't matter how desperately we try to atone for our sins, we will never climb our way back to the garden. This is the ultimate limitation—we cannot fix what we have broken. Paradise is recovered only in being forgiven.

The call for us today is to practice living the unsatisfied life in a satisfying way. How do we do this? It requires three regular habits to put into practice, whether formally or informally. First, become aware of that which is missing in your life. Meditate on it. Enter into it. Imagine getting what you always wanted but you know you can't or shouldn't have or pursue. Second, take stock of your blessings, what you have in your life as a gift. Third, in prayer, give thanks for the blessings, release the object of your longing to God, and ask God to make his grace sufficient to cover what is missing.

On this side of the cross and resurrection, the time has come to recover created dignity to life. The time has come to stand tall again and rejoice. And the time has come to be grateful and let go of the guilt—because God has. But you have to choose to believe that. It is the choice of your life. Amen.

2

The Wesleyan Way of Health-Filled Faith

THE WESLEYAN SCHOLAR ALBERT C. Outler characterized practical eighteenth-century theologian John Wesley's worldview as a quadrilateral, featuring the following four elements, in descending order of importance:

a) Scripture
b) Tradition
c) Reason
d) Experience

These four elements are a staple of practically every branch of Christianity, and they are remarkably helpful in the management of my condition. I wanted to share them with you. Maybe hearing about my self-understanding as a Christian sufferer of SMI will help you grow in yours. See "My Daily Go-To's" in the Appendix for pointers on how to make your own framework. Knowing that I put "My Daily Go-To's" in the Appendix assures me you won't despair if you disagree with what follows.

A. SCRIPTURE

Scripture reminds me that I am not God. Remembering the primacy of Scripture, I learn to be suspicious of thoughts that make me feel exceedingly special. Of course, we are all special, and we are especially made in God's image. But SMI is part of the fallen creation and our fallen human condition. While even those of us with SMI are very special in God's eyes, don't forget that none of us is more special than the other, and Scripture reminds us of that. It also says that the weaker are to be treated with greater care, so take heart in that.

Scripture should be read in community, but this is difficult with some mental illnesses. For me, I can suffer from paranoia, and so sometimes I need to take breaks in my interaction with groups. This was especially the case when I was on less medicine, but I still occasionally need a break, which is why online religious education has been a dream come true for me. Because people are focused on holiness paired with justice in the Nazarene tradition, they are always encouraging and pure-hearted in their interactions with me. Nazarene higher education is my favorite, at least at NNU.

Community is important and Christians are very focused on community to an extent that seems unfair from my vantage point as a sufferer of SMI who wants to do Christianity "right." Community, in whatever capacity that looks like right now given my, at times, challenging condition, is life-saving or traumatic. It depends on the day. Over time, I have grown more confident in trusting myself and stating when I need to step away, and when I need to follow through with staying away even as people urge me to return to community. Being open about my illness helps me manage people's expectations of me, and it makes it less likely that I will emotionally wound people if I suddenly become distant or have to redefine the boundaries of a relationship. Many of my communities are online and, again, I do step away when needed, sometimes ending relationships or redrawing boundaries that ultimately cost me relationships. Prioritizing my relationship with God above my popularity or networking potential has been life-changing.

Reading scripturally and in community is where one experiences consensus and Holy-Spirit-informed reality. Surrendering to this heals my flawed thinking, flawed thinking that I have even learned at church. Not all communities are created equal. What it comes down to is biblical interpretation. There are two types of readers of the Bible, straddling what I call the axis of representation.

We see "reality" (social justice gospel), which gains definition through our discovery of the shortcomings of the "ideal" (holiness fundamentalism that is not responsive to the needs of today). The Bible as a book is the marker of the gap between these methods of importing Scripture into our daily lives. We need bifocal vision to move forward constructively at this time. In short, a Wesleyan, integrated lens. We need to blend social justice with holiness, and to do so in a way that is reasonable and sustainable. This is what biblical scholars mean when they say that true holiness is social holiness.

B. TRADITION

This value is important because there are books written by people with SMI that claim to be authoritative in their treatment of psychiatry, psychology, or theology when really the person is not trained in those fields, and could cause harm writing with false authority to suffering people who will believe anything because they really need help. Some of us even make up blogs about this without stating that we're not professionals. Therefore, let me state it again: I am not writing to you as a professional.

Some writers and speakers will make us feel bad for needing our medicine; some ordained people among them. (I almost died after going off my medicine for a "faith healing" in 2015.)

Some will make us feel damned because we have mental health challenges.

So, this brings me to a related point. When I think about tradition as a person with SMI, I mean tradition bifocally: scientific tradition (which Wesley, writing in the 1700s, called reason) and religious tradition.

I also want to acknowledge the prophetic tradition in this section about tradition. As Revelation teaches, social injustice can be systemic. Our work for systemic change in an unjust world must be done with discernment, and in relationship with communities who are experiencing systemic oppression. I don't want to make this a philosophical tract about social justice, but it would be foolish for me to ignore the fact that people suffering with SMI are also victims of structural oppression, and that people of color and impoverished white people with SMI, including veterans, can be particularly disadvantaged.

There is a strong social justice tradition in Christianity. African-American faith leader Dr. Brenda Salter McNeal has shown that for our witness to be authentic to outsiders of the faith, we cannot ignore social ills like racism (see her book *A Credible Witness*). This is true even if we are feeling particularly oppressed as people with SMI. I learned the hard way that talking about how I was oppressed as a person with SMI, and how much I suffered too, was counterproductive to the justice for which I was advocating. Dr. Salter McNeil's more recent book (*Becoming Brave*) shows that social ills must be addressed structurally and, at times, politically. We cannot spiritualize injustice. We are bodies making up the body of Christ and not just souls.

In his book *Truth Therapy*, the middle portion of which I use as a devotional every morning,[1] Dr. Peter Bellini rightly talks about how racism is a cognitive distortion that can be remedied with the Bible and faithful study of the passages he provides in the book. Let's not forget, though, that it's not just a cognitive distortion but also a bodily distortion, that can kill people of color. Resmaa Menakem argues that non-white bodies, not just brains, have been conditioned to perceive African-American bodies as a threat. It is visceral, says Menakem, who himself is an African-American man who works as a body therapist with both violent offenders and police officers (who can also, though by no means always, be violent offenders themselves).

Jesus was *bodily* crucified. We can't forget this. I read Menekem's book *My Grandmother's Hands* every morning and it has deepened my willingness to believe people of color when they describe their experiences of racism, and then to *act* compassionately and disruptively in favor of justice. My quality of eye contact with people of color is noticeably improved on days when I go through the exercises Menekem describes in his book.

---

1. See "My Daily Go-To's" in the Appendix for more details.

It is a matter not only of social health but also of mental health to remember that our souls are in bodies while we are on this earth. I will talk more about this in the reason and experience sections that follow.

C. REASON

Now this one—reason—marks Wesley as a man of the eighteenth century, leading up to the Enlightenment. The primacy of "lived experience" is what the liberals often advocate for, and it is not enough. We also must be rational, which is a perspective traditionally ascribed to the conservatives. Because of this, I often put reason and experience together: you need both to be balanced. But this also has implications for SMI, where reason and experience can both become disordered, burdensome, and perhaps even deadly. SMI impacts both our reason and our experience. In fact, people will kindly refer to us as "experiencing" mental illness. This is the nicest way to say it because then we're not labeling a person with a permanent label of "mentally ill."

When I'm experiencing symptoms of SMI, my illness history triggers my reasoning capabilities on a meta-level: I know I need to take my medicine, avoid stress, and, given that I find it healing to share about my illness, share with safe people that they should not to take my behavior seriously as a reflection of my best self, apologizing and repairing harm wherever possible.

(By the way, the more consistent I became with professional help and *medicine*, the more I studied the fruit of the spirit, and the more I studied Scripture generally, the less often I harmed people. I have never harmed people physically, but I have harmed people emotionally. Sometimes, when we're just getting our dosages settled in, we can be more agitated than previously. For me, it took four years to get on the right dosage, but I never gave up hope, and neither should you.)

D. EXPERIENCE

Experience is the trickiest for me, which is why I'm glad that the scholar of Wesley I mentioned earlier, Outler, put reason ahead of experience in the quadrilateral. I have experienced what is clinically termed a "lack of insight"; meaning that I experienced myself as being fine and normal, while really, I was putting myself in serious harm and almost died from my behavior. I have compassion for those who have harmed others while ill, but only if they commit to nonviolence, get in treatment, and stay with it. SMI can make people dangerous to themselves and/or others. Don't give us a bad name as peaceful sufferers of SMI, please.

I was hospitalized involuntarily once. It was traumatic and impacted me for years, so I'm not going to talk about it here, but this is why we need to stay on medicine. We often cannot trust our experience. SMI, in some ways, is an experiential illness. I have little signs, like if I'm shaking my leg, it means I need to get up and stretch, take a shower, or stop doing whatever I'm doing because I'm starting to leave my body. Or sometimes I'll wake up really early and think, "Oh, imagine how much I could get done if I got up now!" But then I am reminded that I need to keep a regular sleep schedule and just lay in bed until a reasonable hour, trusting that I'm training myself in good habits for the long haul, prioritizing long-term wellness, social and moral accountability, and responsibility. In this way, I strive to maintain a solid Christian witness.

Also related to the experience quadrant: I will say that I have mystical experiences and feel heavily the anointing of the Holy Spirit, often, even as I write this. Some of this may be due to SMI; in fact, secular mental health therapists would definitely say that that was the case. I've heard of pregnant women thinking that they were birthing the Messiah, and of men thinking that they were Jesus. They felt it down to their very bones, experientially. But Scripture, reason, tradition, and the Christian community clearly contradict that experience. That's why all four need to be together.

ALL FOUR, TOGETHER

Scripture, tradition, reason, and experience, together, in that order, help me to balance out and, I would argue, also help keep me healthy in the first place. If we could raise our children attentive to all four aspects from day one, think about the resourcefulness and godliness that would follow for future generations; however, it should be remembered that there are many children who grow up to develop SMI who had great parents. Some therapists build rapport with clients by emphasizing the client's total innocence, regardless of whether or not this is actually the case.

Children *do* experience serious familial and social problems as if they are the cause of them, so it's not wrong to acknowledge that we begin life as innocent beings who can be harmed irreparably. But take it too far and this wisdom can prove disempowering. We don't want to forget the first chapter of this book: never let anyone take away your dignity of making a choice for your life. Don't only see yourself as a victim, even if you are a victim. Try to move into the survivor category, which includes removing yourself (and any children) from abusive people and situations, and seeking immediate mental health treatment if you are physically or sexually abusing anyone, or if you have developed a chemical or sexual addiction. There is help out there. It's a journey that is essential for Christians or potential Christians.

3

An Integrated, Christian Worldview

CULTURE IS A BEING, just like aspen groves, sequoias, coral reefs, and flocks of birds, which fly across the sky in their predictable patterns—and American culture is broken. Piety and the development of spiritual disciplines are not enough in a broken culture. The Bible teaches that every culture can be broken. In fact, on this side of heaven it's a given. Luckily, the Bible also teaches that we have a God who seeks to mend it and to reconcile us to himself. It is relationship as process, not stasis. The story of the Old Testament is the story of God's persistence in seeking to establish, and then to maintain, a covenant relationship with Israel. The Gospels teach us that Christ died to make the covenant permanent and unbreakable, but that we still have our own free will, and are able to reject it.

The church is called to disciple people to be authentic witnesses to the redeeming love of Christ. Discipleship does not entail people making clones of themselves. We are each born with different callings, different personalities, and different ways of being in the world; that is beautiful and what God intended. The fruit of discipleship should be seen as striving for justice and acts of mercy, because this is what Jesus did.

Let's look in this chapter about what this means for mental health and public health.

Our health care system in the United States is functioning poorly. We are not attending to the spiritual aspect of our problems, in health care or even in the church. My afterword talks about how we are not invested in a holistic approach to education either. It is all connected. We are not holistic in the United States, but, rather, we are atomized. In first drafts of this book, some commenters remarked that it was odd that I had incorporated social justice—the thing is, that marks their thinking as atomized, too. We are to be integrated and realistic Christians. I am proposing a Christian realism that doesn't forget that as Christians in America we are historically situated in a world marked by poverty and injustice, including racial injustice.

There must be a merging of piety and justice, and there is no real spiritual sustenance without food on the table. In communities that don't have reliable access to healthy food, known as "food deserts," to name just one example of how health intersects with community health, especially with communities of color, but also amongst poor white families, communities that don't have healthy options for food acquire bad eating habits and poor mental and physical health. What you eat matters for mental health. But if the only thing to eat is fast food because you are located in low-income areas without grocery stores and farmers' markets, and are experiencing the cumulative effects of our history of civilian-initiated and government-supported segregation, then there is a problem (read *The Color of Law* for a full account). And if you're working long hours and can't afford gas, that is another hardship.

The abandonment of entire swaths of our nation, like the African-American community in Flint, Michigan, is a tragedy. There are recent books that also document the so-called "deaths of despair" in the white community as well, for example the books *Tightrope* (for a liberal take) or *Hillbilly Elegy* (for a conservative take). It comes from a systemic failure to address basic human needs, paired with utter disregard for the impact of business policy on the environment.

A lot of youth anxiety stems from worries about the environment that we adults have become so used to that they don't dominate our thinking consistently. When I was teaching reading at a local elementary school, the children started crying as we read about polar bears, even though the book I was reading from didn't talk about their current crisis as the globe warms—they just had an automatic association between polar bears and extinction. The children also provided many other examples of animals and forests that were endangered. It is top of mind for the younger generations especially.

Under such neglectful conditions, mental health challenges flourish. The ignorance, willful or no, of the privileged to the plight of those who feed our wallets, and our unwillingness to take partial responsibility for it, lead to the mental distortions that accompany the faith lives of the rich, who don't see their riches as something to be shared or leveraged for justice and the flourishing of American society and the world. Sometimes, when we are generous, we make it about ourselves, our charity, and our goodness, rather than making it about justice.

There is also the opioid crisis here in the States, and the spread of addictions and other behavioral challenges. It is all connected.

Our culture, as I said above, is not a creation but a being. And the Christian form of that being is the body of Christ, in other words the church, as described by the apostle Paul. Jesus says that he is the vine and we are the branches. Branches should have no part in cutting other branches from the vine of Christ and the fullness of a Christian life. The state of the poor in the United States, the poor of all colors, including the systemic injustice suffered by the African-American and Indigenous communities, and the economic exploitation of people of color generally, mark us as a challenging place to live for many of the people who live within our borders.

As Christians, when we don't work for justice—there are many ways to right wrongs—we are falling short of God's will for our lives. We must repent, and after repentance comes a soul change that manifests in meaningful social action. I will say of our leaders that there is a special suffering that comes from thinking that to succeed is to forego taking responsibility. Responsibility, especially moral responsibility, is the fruit of authentic Scripture study in community (or discipleship), and authentic discipleship, in turn, makes for authentic witnessing, which, in turn, leads to not only personal holiness but social holiness. Ultimately, more are attracted to Christ's church in a way that is sustainable when our witness is credible, in other words, when we are socially responsible. That means holding leaders accountable and urging them to be morally responsible as well.

When we acknowledge the realities of our context as Americans, our discipleship becomes authentic. Christ again becomes the head of the church and not our egos or our country. Not nationalism or ethnocentrism, which deprive us, even Christians, of our humanity.

Also, if we are not people of color ourselves, how our white leaders talk about other populations reflects on us as white people. We should have no tolerance for racism, bigotry, or ethnocentrism.

Regardless of our political stance on immigration matters, we must never forget that humans are made in the image of God. No human being is illegal; for a human to be illegal would mean that they weren't made in the image of God. We are *all* created in the image of God.

4

Recovering Dignity and Hope

IF CULTURE IS AN organism, then the nature of that organism, the health of that organism, is rooted in religion. All problems can be traced back to religion, religious belief, or the lack thereof. Religion is the foundation of the human mind, and it reflects the divine truth that there is in fact a God, who was the father of Jesus, and that Jesus, in turn, was with God at the beginning and will be at the end. He is the alpha and the omega. A prophet's prophet. The culmination of the prophets and the perfecter of their message. The embodiment of that message of salvation, salvation by a loving God who sacrificed his Son for the sake of the world.

As Christians, our voices are not merely a physical aspect of our having a body. Rather, they are something to be grown into and owned. Voices are how we reach our audience, and how we evangelize the world. To do this well requires discipleship of not just our voices but of our bodies. And we must be discipled into becoming a credible witness, and that includes prophetic witness and alleviation of current social ills that are taking place not just spiritually, but also bodily. Social injustice is foremost among the ills in our country and the world.

But there are also the universal sins of the flesh.

The integrity of our voices defines our status as Christians, and with SMI, my "voice"—my witness—was damaged. But this began in secular education, where I was not discipled in Christ but was, rather, discipled in the ways of the world. I became interested in another man while married, while studying art, specifically literature and film, that promoted sexual immorality. Not all people who suffer from bipolar disorder are sexually immoral or unfaithful, though it is frequently the case that sexual impulses and experiences can be stronger. Though this is a symptom of people's illnesses when they suffer from bipolar disorder (and schizoaffective disorder is affiliated with bipolar disorder), I still had to learn to take responsibility for my misplaced affections as well. I couldn't just be impure and blame it on the illness. (This is another reason why taking medication is important with SMI: our impulses are brought under control.) What happened in my sin wasn't just my fault, and in reflecting I have determined that I could have been more forthcoming about how I was wronged since power abuse was also a factor; but it is no longer my battle and so I'm not going to write about it here.

Acknowledging my sin was the first step in recovering. And I confessed to God and my husband and was forgiven by both. Forgiving the others involved was the next step. Forgiving myself was the final step.

There is a self-compassion movement that centers on acknowledging our transgressions and accepting them and ourselves. This is far from what Christ calls us to. We are not supposed to stay mired in sin; nor are we supposed to look at our past transgressions with pride, complacency, or self-assurance. We repent, are cleansed, *and change course*, taking medicine as prescribed, which can deepen our ability to keep our commitments to ourselves and loved ones. In my case, and I think this is what we *must* do as Christians, I relied on being first forgiven by Christ, and then I forgave myself and the people who wronged me (and whom I wronged). Most of all, I am grateful to my wonderful husband, Todd. I love him tremendously and will never let him down again.

Ezekiel 37, a portion of which is featured in my epigraph, was written in the sixth century BCE while Ezekiel was living with fellow Judeans in Babylonian exile. It was a hopeless time. The first half of the book of Ezekiel is set before the fall of Jerusalem, but by the time we get to this passage Jerusalem has fallen and the temple has been destroyed. God says to Ezekiel, "Son of man, these bones are the whole house of Israel. Listen to what they're saying: 'Our bones are dried up, our hope is gone, there's nothing left of us'" (Ezekiel 37:11). In the original Hebrew this actually rhymes, which has the effect of making their despair ring longer in your ears. But in the original Hebrew that phrase "our hope is lost" can also be rendered "our hope has perished." The word here for "to cut off" when I read "we are cut off completely," it actually means "to be destroyed" and in some contexts the same verb can refer to one who has died and been buried.

This makes it so that the plaint is something like this: "Our bones are dried up, and our hope has perished; we have died and been buried." It is not an exaggeration to read it this way.

We all have moments in life that have dried us up, down to the very bones. Life will do that to us sometimes. I once read about a woman named Faith, and about her valley of bones, the death of her young husband from appendicitis that was misdiagnosed. The man died young in spite of having been taken to the doctor's. She told them something was wrong, and they sent him home anyway. She was beside herself, confident he was dying, and no one would listen, and then he died.[1]

Now if that's not the valley of dry bones, I don't know what is.

She experienced panic attacks, suicidal thoughts, was prescribed psychiatric medications, had flashbacks, and was haunted by the constant question, "How could they have sent me home with a dying man?"

What Faith experienced on a personal level, and what those of us who suffer deeply experience, is akin to what Israel experienced collectively. Let me explain.

There is so much more at work in Ezekiel 37 than death and despair. This is a passage people have turned to for centuries for inspiration, actually.

---

1. This story comes from Zimbardo et al., *Time Cure*.

In this passage, we can see the very seeds of the resurrection, when God commands Ezekiel to prophesy to Israel, "Therefore, prophesy. Tell them, 'God, the Master, says: I'll dig up your graves and bring you out alive—O my people! Then I'll take you straight to the land of Israel. When I dig up graves and bring you out as my people, you'll realize that I am God. I'll breathe my life into you and you'll live. Then I'll lead you straight back to your land and you'll realize that I am God. I've said it and I'll do it. God's Decree'" (Ezekiel 37:12–14).

You see, this passage isn't about the valley of bones. This passage is about what God *does* with the valley of bones. It's about what God does with our valley of bones, our despair, when we feel like we have no hope, when we feel cut off, dead and buried. He doesn't leave us where Proverbs leaves us, with good medicine if we're happy already and with despair and death when we're downtrodden and feel as though we have just died.

Faith is lifted out of her valley of bones by faith, therapy, and medication, and the people who surround her over a long journey that spanned several years. I would be the last person to tell you that with enough faith we will be spared the valley of dry bones. We walk through the valley of the shadow of death in this life.

What this passage is asking us to do is live into our bones, even in the valley. May we keep Ezekiel's message in our hearts. May we sit in the valley of dry bones and to live into it, trusting that God sends the Spirit into the valleys of our lives and that our suffering will be redeemed. Indeed, that it already is being redeemed.

But how to be assured that all shall be well when it is not well right now?

5

A Wesleyan Vitamin

I WANTED TO BOOKEND this work with the wisdom of ordained clergy. If my pastor, whose sermon I opened with, was the one who helped me to accept and even thrive within my limitations, to the extent where I ultimately realized that we all have them, Dr. Steele's worldview as a Wesleyan professor of moral and historical theology helped me find meaning and purpose even in the act of taking medicine. I had an early psychiatrist who recommended I that consider taking my medicine to be like taking a vitamin. That was helpful. But getting a Christian vitamin through a Wesleyan lens has been absolutely transformational for my quality of life and my self-concept, and it has inspired my eagerness to learn more about Wesley and to be a faithful disciple in alignment with the Wesleyan tradition.

In their book *Christian Ethics and Nursing Practice*, Drs. Steele and Monroe outline their whole worldview through a biblical lens that features the four moral strands of biblical discourse: law, holiness, wisdom, and prophecy. I especially recommend this book to anyone who is in the nursing profession or who is caring for a person with chronic illness, even SMI. It provides wisdom and gives meaning to the task of caring for others as a way of living out our calling to Jesus Christ.

MY THOUGHTS WITHIN A YEAR
OF BEING HOSPITALIZED

June 16, 2016

Dear Professor Steele,

The role of choice in your worldview disturbs me to the core as a Christian because it makes me feel I have no free will if not on my medicine, because if off my medicine I'm running the risk of not perceiving things "accurately" enough to make logical choices in the first place. I can't help but wonder if this importance of agency in your worldview is the result of Enlightenment or historicist thinking or not, but at least from my disability's viewpoint, free will is not always exercisable. Does this mean that I am not able to cultivate virtues consistently enough to be worthy of the kingdom of heaven? Does this mean I am sometimes possessed by the devil? I have never harmed anyone. I don't indulge in vices as much as the average American, but I'm surely committing some accidentally.

Best wishes,

Erin

Hi Erin,

I do not regard "free will" primarily as doing what you want, but as wanting what you ought. Of course, you aren't free if you can't do what you want, but you also aren't free if your wants are disordered. And there are many things that can disorder a person's desires: abusive upbringing, physical illness, insufficient education, a wide array of morally and intellectually corrosive social forces, and so on. And disordered desires are dehumanizing. Conversely, there are many things that can help a person to align his or her desires with human nature—that is, our nature as revealed, redeemed and healed by the Incarnate Son of God. To the extent that our desires and priorities are rightly ordered, we come closer and closer to being who we truly are, who we are truly "meant to be." Of course, this presupposes that we have access to a normative account of human life (i.e., Christian Scripture and tradition, taken *en bloc*) and an array of elucidating examples (i.e., the lives of the saints).

Many years ago, a member of the congregation that Marilyn and I were then co-pastoring was committed to a psychiatric ward. I can't recall now what his diagnosis was, but I do remember that when I visited him, I was told by the nurses that his mental condition was deteriorating because he wasn't taking his meds. So, I met with him, and after the usual pleasantries I told him the nurses had informed me that he was resisting taking his meds, and asked him why. He said that doing so would be a sin, because it would show his lack of faith in God's healing power. I asked him whether he believed that God works "in nature." Yes, he said, the Bible teaches that. Then I asked him whether he believes that God works "in human history." Again, he agreed that that claim was scriptural.

So, then I asked, "Well, then, what's to keep God from working through medical science, which constitutes the sum total of human efforts to cooperate with God's intention to help us flourish?"

"I hadn't considered that," he said. "I guess you're right."

That day he resumed his meds, and a week later he was discharged from the hospital and started rebuilding his life. The point here is that my friend wasn't truly free when he was refusing to take his meds, because something was impeding his ability to understand and receive the healing that God wills. True, he was exercising human agency of a sort by refusing his meds; but the act of refusing was itself a function of his disordered understanding of the life of faith and of a confused and self-destructive way of being in the world. Once he felt free to take his meds without injuring his conscience, he was freed by the meds from some of his confused thinking, disordered priorities, and self-destructive illusions, and able to get back in the game of living.

Warm Regards,

RBS

2 YEARS LATER: THE FRIENDSHIP CONTINUES

May 30, 2018

Dear Rick,

I found an article that explains perfectly who I am. I experience chronic ego diffusion, don't have a sense of self, and instead have a series of as-if personalities as I take on the narratives of others. There's an article about it. I kind of wish I hadn't found it. Please read it and pray for me.

Erin

Hi Erin,

I'm not quite sure why you wish you hadn't found this article, unless it is that you find what looks like a "perfect explanation of who you are" very uncomfortable to read. If that is the reason, then let me remind you of three things:

First, medical diagnoses, and especially psychiatric diagnoses, are composite pictures of doctors' observations of many patients, which exist to help other doctors, who observe similar phenomena in their patients proceed therapeutically. That is, they are guides to asking good questions during therapy session and to prescribing helpful medications. For those purposes, they are very useful.

But second, no actual patient is ever "perfectly explained" by even the most accurate medical diagnosis. Clinically, human beings cannot be reduced—and ethically human beings *must* not be reduced—to "cases" of one or more medical conditions. The "patient" is a person first, last, and always, and a diagnosis provides his or her doctor with clinical strategies for minimizing the number of mistakes the doctor makes in treating that person.

And third, from the perspective of the patient, the medical diagnosis can also be useful in self-understanding. But complete self-understanding—assuming that is ever possible—is always more than the sum total of the diagnosable medical conditions from which one suffers. Which is a roundabout way of saying, keep working on your book. Your book may be all the better for illustrating the way in which a condition called "schizophrenia" (or whatever) manifests itself in your behavior and relationships, and shapes your personal and professional life. But the book I want to read is not a book about "schizophrenia." It's a book about Erin, who happens to have schizophrenia, but who also loves Russian novels, throws great parties, is married to a wonderful guy named Todd, is a staunch defender of LGBTQIA+ folks, has a close personal relationship with Gautama Buddha[1] and Jesus of Nazareth, etc., etc., I couldn't deduce any of those other important things about my friend Erin from the fact that I know she struggles with schizophrenia. Nor would I properly know Erin if I knew only about her psychiatric condition, and knew nothing about her party-throwing skills, her literary tastes, her political and religious convictions, etc. And if I may riff a bit on something you yourself said so beautifully in your previous post, the only way to defeat the dehumanizing pictures of "persons-with-mental-illness" that we get in the media is if those persons tell their own stories, in rich detail, and show that there is more to them . . . much more . . . than some diagnostic category.

Praying, as always, for you and Todd,
Rick

Rick—Thanks so much. I really cherish you. I am deeply moved by your response. This will help me greatly with my faith and with my ability to believe more literally what the Bible says because now I know my tendency to explore and contradict comes from deep within my mind and is not a reflection of the truth of the Gospel as humans are meant to experience it. All my qualifications are from a mind that lacks unity. But Paul says we are clay vessels and if I'm an empty one then the best thing to fill it with is the Bible and becoming a conduit of the spirit through the Bible's teaching, or more precisely, Jesus'. I let the spirit move through me and act selflessly most of the time, and I now see why it is easier for me to do this. I have a fragmented identity and very little instinct towards self-preservation (unless I'm protecting my fragile mind).

It is also depressing to realize from this description that I'm probably like this not only from seizures, which I think played a

1. I no longer identify as a Buddhist, though I respect Buddhism's insights into the human condition.

major role, but also because of other traumas I've encountered in life. This makes me sad. Thanks for being one of the best dads I know. I really needed these words.

Appendix, aka Breadcrumbs

Overview

THE APPENDIX FEATURES WHAT readers have said have been my most helpful blog posts over the years. I want to remind you that I am writing from my own lived experience and am not claiming that my experience will be like yours or anyone else's. My own experience of my own illness varies by the year itself. Sometimes hearing one person's openness is healing to another, even if that other person's path will end up being different. With the following entries, I offer breadcrumbs from my own path, which itself may change over the years. Never give up hope! I personally think we should always have our hearts open to remission if not a full recovery, while committing to always take at least some medicine. Everyone has their own path.

a. How to Interact with People in Crisis

Here's what I want: Give me a God-listening heart
so I can lead your people well, discerning the differ-
ence between good and evil. For who on their own
is capable of leading your glorious people?

—*1 KINGS 3:9*

A FRIEND OF MINE has been distressed and so we've been talking
more than usual lately. They asked me if I could talk to their family
about how to treat them when they're having a hard time because
I'm such a good listener and their family only freaks them out or
makes them angry. To which I said: "First of all, please tell my husband that you think I'm a good listener! He'll be amazed!"

I will share two things from people who supported me during
my dark period in my late twenties that I channel when talking to
my struggling friend on the phone:

First, to use an expression from teaching, I show them unconditional positive regard. This means that no matter what the friend
says I continue to view them as fully human and worthy of love
and respect, and I don't take what they say personally if they get
triggered by my reaction. I treat this, instead, as more information
about how to interact with them in the future. (Obviously there are
some things that need reporting, like any ideas of causing harm to
people or self—*never* keep this kind of thing confidential and never
leave a person who is suicidal unattended. Obviously if they are
violent or dangerous, leave).

And second, I never push them to give me more information than they're sharing. I just repeat back with some variation what they've already said with genuine feeling and interest to show that I'm listening, that I care, and that I want to hear more if they want to share. This is so important, especially if the person is experiencing paranoia, that you are not pushing them to share more than they want, which will just make them more anxious, paranoid, and isolated.

Honestly, I recommend taking classes or talking to a therapist about how you can help your loved one since every person with mental illness is mentally ill in their own way. I'm just sharing my experience here.

And know that things may not be this hard forever! The brain changes! Especially with medical help and therapy! And if you take some therapy to help yourself cope then it will greatly help your family unit.

b. The Dark Side: Overcoming It

So here's what I want you to do, God helping you: Take your everyday, ordinary life—your sleeping, eating, going-to-work, and walking-around life—and place it before God as an offering. Embracing what God does for you is the best thing you can do for him. Don't become so well-adjusted to your culture that you fit into it without even thinking. Instead, fix your attention on God. You'll be changed from the inside out. Readily recognize what he wants from you, and quickly respond to it. Unlike the culture around you, always dragging you down to its level of immaturity, God brings the best out of you, develops well-formed maturity in you.

—ROMANS 12:1–2

EVERYONE HAS A DARK side, but if you don't encounter difficulty, you don't usually know this about yourself. People who lack compassion, in my experience, either forget that they have a dark side, or they are living from this dark side and can't even begin to see the light that would be possible if they went into therapy, exercised, and perhaps humbled themselves to the LORD.

If we think people think poorly of us, then typically we will either be defiant and consider ourselves "oppressed" (even if we're the ones being problematic), or . . . we may become the "bad" person people think we are. We will act out their expectations of us because we see ourselves only how they see us (or think they see us). This is very true if we don't have a strong sense of self. Which is why, if you're really struggling, it is important to surround yourself with loving, nonjudgmental, and hopeful people.

Another thing can happen: we sometimes imagine that others think poorly of us when really, they've already moved on! Don't forget that this might also be the case!

Christian faith illumines our way out like nothing else does:

If we continue to look outside of ourselves for approval and find rejection, we despair without Christ who reminds us that we are strongest when we learn from our weaknesses and lean on him. We must ask Christ to give us our identity and not our job; our goodness to our fellow humans in spite their rejection of us, and not our popularity.

We must stop looking horizontally, which means focusing on the people around us who we imagine judging us, and instead look vertically, upward to God and then, through him, go on to the work that we are called to do. I think a lot of school and workplace shootings happen when people look horizontally and obsess over where they stand in relationship to society, rather than upward to their relationship to themselves, their God, and their consciences. We are to dig down deeper into God in our peril and forget the ways of the world, our reputations, and what the world thinks of us. And act justly even, actually especially, when people expect otherwise.

Just because you're rejected doesn't make you like Christ. Being harmless in the face of oppression, rejection, and harm posed by others, even our very friends, makes us like Christ.

c. What Is Psychosis Like?

I don't think the way you think.
The way you work isn't the way I work.
God's Decree.

—ISAIAH 55:9

UNFORTUNATELY, THE NATURE OF psychosis is such that people by definition do not have insight into what is happening to them. Insight is a clinical term. It means that you can see that you are suffering. A person with OCD, for example, will often know that what they are doing is not "normal" or desirable. Not so for psychosis. A story comes to mind just now to illustrate the point:

My grandfather, Ross, played polo competitively as a young man. One game he was struck by a mallet and lost his eye. Being in shock, he didn't know this had happened to him initially, and he wondered why the men around him were fainting off of their horses when they looked at him. He felt fine. What was the big deal?!?

Fast forward to me in graduate school: I'm doing fine!!! Why are people so suspicious of me and not willing to hang out with me? Why are they being compassionate?!? Why does it seem like they pity me?!?

People experience psychosis and have fully functioning families and careers all the time. No one talks about it! But the first time . . .—even if we do sense that something is amiss, no one wants to admit it might be happening to *them*.

And the vast majority of people do not know that it is treatable. It took years for me to find the right medicine and mindset. But I never gave up, and neither should you.

This denial about becoming ill is just natural human behavior. For example, some people also experience shock at a cancer diagnosis, or disbelief when they are in a serious car crash. This is a natural, universal aspect of getting a devastating diagnosis or of surviving horrific events. It is so natural and we must be compassionate with ourselves and with others when we are struck with bad news and know that it is natural to be taken aback and be incredulous that horrible things can happen to us.

It is natural human behavior to deny what is going on and, in the case of mental health, to not want to accept help, realize that you can, or trust that it will work out if you do. But we must never give up hope, and we must not be afraid to seek help. Medicine made me well and made it so I could keep up my career and stay in my relationships. So did therapy. So did ending toxic relationships and finding God and putting him in place of the idols of career and popularity.

d. Change to Heal

God's a safe-house for the battered,
a sanctuary during bad times.
The moment you arrive, you relax;
you're never sorry you knocked.

—PSALM 9:9–10

ASK YOURSELF:

Am I committed to getting better?

Is there something I am getting from being ill?

What steps am I willing to take to improve?

There is always a chance we have an investment in staying ill
. . . and often we hide this from ourselves.

Ask yourself:

Am I taking responsibility for myself?

Am I thinking of others?

Am I committed to my treatment?

Am I praying for others?

Am I being humble?

Never forget that, no matter what, we must love ourselves as
we *are* to get better, but we also must be willing and open to *change*.

e. Feeling Feelings and Not Fighting Them

*I'll never forget the trouble, the utter lostness, the
taste of ashes, the poison I've swallowed. I remember
it all—oh, how well I remember—the feeling of hit-
ting the bottom. But there's one other thing I remember, and remembering, I keep a grip on hope ...*

—LAMENTATIONS 3:19–21

JESUS IS CARRYING US when we suffer most. This is hard to remember because often, when we are struggling, people urge us forward.
Get up! Go on with your day! Let's move!

Yes, I say. And yet . . . sometimes when we allow ourselves to
feel, to really feel our feelings rather than fight through them, peace
follows.

Knock and the door will be opened to you . . . Ask and it will
be granted . . .

Yes, I say. And yet . . . sometimes we don't get what we want.
How can we be grateful for our pain and disappointment?

What always helped me when I was having a hard time was
to look at myself as if from above, as a loving person would look at
their beloved child. As God would look at one of his creations that
was struggling . . . With pity and concern is how he looks at us when
we are struggling.

And out of the valley of bones, a place of despair, comes the
message that Jesus carrying us in our suffering. That he is carrying
us. And that we are not forgotten. If you are being carried by God,

that means that you are his beloved child, and that all shall be well, if not in this life, then the next one.

Jesus is carrying us when we suffer most.

f. What Are Antipsychotics Like? In Two Parts

Be alert servants of the Master, cheerfully expectant.

—ROMANS 12:12

PART 1: MASKED LIFE—WHAT I LOST . . .

What do I tell myself when my face is a mask?

I tell myself that I am still me and that my soul still shines from within my body, even if its center is now the heart and not the eyes. Even if my eyes cannot sparkle and the wrinkles around my eyes do not respond immediately to the interactions I have on a day-to-day basis, I remind myself that I am still me, that my heart is full of love and compassion and I that I still matter to God.

Being on antipsychotics is hard initially. Everyone is different and so I merely share my own experience:

It changes your whole personality and you only very slowly learn how to accept the fact that you cannot command the room the way you did when you were hyper, sparky, and sparkly. Your feet drag, your face doesn't move except with great effort. Conversations lose their immediacy and you feel less persuasive. You flex your jaw, even when you're not chewing. Your tongue moves. You are in a fog.

"You look over-medicated, Erin," an abrasive colleague once shouted across the office at the school where I was working. I had confided in a different colleague that I was on medication and this was how I learned that everyone now knew this about me.

But I was numb from my medicine and so this didn't even sting. I lost my glimmer as a motivational speaker and high-impact teacher. My relationships with my students became strained. And eventually, I had to leave the teaching profession because I had lost the love and effortlessness of teaching groups.

PART 2: THRIVING ANYWAY— WHAT I GAINED . . .

Trust of others, because I was not volatile.

Confidence, because I was perceiving reality accurately.

Community, because I had the ability to make appointments because I could trust that I would keep them and that I would be well for them.

Safety. Because I felt safe and was safe.

The ability to trust myself. Self-reliance.

Employment. I found my calling helping others.

The relief of my husband who could finally relax.

Continuity. My life narrative.

My parents, with whom I had stopped talking because I had imagined all sorts of things that hadn't really happened in my childhood and was angry at them.

Resolve. I read Elyn Saks's *The Center Cannot Hold* about her persistence in the face of a severe case of schizophrenia, and took heart that she had survived and that that meant that I could, too.

And through this, too, I found . . . community. A more authentic community than I had ever known. The knowledge that many are on antipsychotics and live fully functioning lives, and the pride in knowing that some of us even have prestigious careers.

g. Snapping Out of It Is Bad

Anyone who meets a testing challenge head-on and manages to stick it out is mighty fortunate. For such persons loyally in love with God, the reward is life and more life.

—JAMES 1:12

"SNAP OUT OF IT!"

I've been well for several years now, but I didn't just "snap out of it." In this post I talk about why it would be bad to snap out of suffering and how we can help people who are suffering see the bright side. Hint: it's not what you think!

Know this: it is impossible to "snap out" of SMI. And actually, even people who suffer from less officially "serious" mental health issues cannot just "snap out" of them; many do well to seek professional attention. But that's not what this post is about.

Did you know that telling someone to snap out of their woes is terrible, terrible advice, let alone whether this is even possible or not?

People should not just stay in a pit, suffer and wait until they suddenly feel better and can act independently again! Usually this is not even possible.

But I'm saying that even if they could, I would stop them from snapping out of it completely. Because by "snapping out of it" we miss the valleys that helps us grow.

"No pain, no gain" is a horrible expression—never use it! And yet this phrase wouldn't be around if there wasn't some truth behind it.

We must treat pain as our teacher.

In my own case, pain has taught me what matters in life. To me, what matters is helping people who are suffering.

The apostle Paul teaches us about the importance of our dying to our outermost self—the bragging self—the *what's my resume look like?* self. Because what is inside is being transformed when this happens into something glorious. And that wouldn't happen if we could just "snap out of it":

> So we're not giving up. How could we! Even though on the outside it often looks like things are falling apart on us, on the inside, where God is making new life, not a day goes by without his unfolding grace. These hard times are small potatoes compared to the coming good times, the lavish celebration prepared for us. There's far more here than meets the eye. The things we see now are here today, gone tomorrow. But the things we can't see now will last forever. (2 Corinthians 4:16–18)

I would add to the apostle Paul's assertion that just as things which are seen are temporary, that things which are felt are also temporary. We must always remind ourselves that we are not our feelings and we are bigger than how we feel. Always!

How might we help loved ones who are suffering to see this very real bright side to their suffering? How can we frame this for the person so that they can see how they could grow from this?!? How lucky they are?!? How exciting to find something positive! The silver lining!!!!

Alas, we can't make anyone see it. We can only hold space for them to find it out for themselves.

Unfortunately, it is easy to provide encouragement by forcing collective wisdom like "no pain, no gain" or "every cloud has a silver lining" on people who are suffering. I say unfortunately because it's not long after we have done this that we have alienated the person we had meant to help. They probably won't trust us with their pain again! And they'll be still more isolated for it!

I will conclude with an example from my own experience.

I remember how, while stuck in the bleakest despair, my grandma once gave me a gratitude journal and told me to find something to be grateful for everyday and write it down. It's not so bad! Indeed, from the outside things looked great still. To *her!*

The practice of looking for the good could not have been further from my mind. The thought of it repulsed me and I threw the journal in the trash, determined not to fit into the stereotype of the shallow Californian superficially pretending that all was well when I felt like crap. Life went on. (By the way, it's not only Californians who do this . . .) Several months later my mom bought me a gratitude jar. Mom instructed me to write on a piece of paper something to be grateful for every day and then to put it in the jar. And then she backed away and left.

Hmmm. . . . This felt different . . .

. . . Because she did not press me on it, and because she did not lecture me on how important it was to be grateful . . . because she did not "should" on me and say, "you should be grateful!"

. . . Because she did not ask me again, let alone daily, if I was doing what she had recommended . . . or remind me that so-and-so had it worse because they had problem *X* . . .

Because of all of this, I did not throw it away. No—while I did not use the jar—I'm too much of a contrarian for that—still I did not throw it away. And then something amazing happened.

Somehow, over the course of a few months, I began to feel, and eventually to know, that that empty jar was waiting for me for when I would be ready to fill it. It became my space for hope. This was completely unconscious.

And, with time, I visualized myself being able to put notes in it. And eventually I did just that.

Remember, as the apostle Paul wrote in 2 Corinthians 4:18, "The things we see now are here today, gone tomorrow. But the things we can't see now will last forever."

Don't give up hope.

Amen.

h. Accepting Your Diagnosis, Maintaining Hope for Recovery

Summing it all up, friends, I'd say you'll do best by filling your minds and meditating on things true, noble, reputable, authentic, compelling, gracious—the best, not the worst; the beautiful, not the ugly; things to praise, not things to curse. Put into practice what you learned from me, what you heard and saw and realized. Do that, and God, who makes everything work together, will work you into his most excellent harmonies.

—PHILIPPIANS 4:8–9

"WHAT A RELIEF TO finally have a name for my suffering!"

Few who receive a stigmatizing mental health diagnosis utter these words. A bad diagnosis can make what seemed like just a really bad summer a never-ending lifelong sentence of despair. If this applies to you, take heart! This does not have to be the case! Diagnoses, though helpful, cause harm unless you frame them differently than most doctors will. Read on to hear what I did to bring healing and hope back to my life in spite of my diagnosis.

It has been said that the body achieves what the mind believes. Our minds are incredibly powerful and they shape our reality and our futures, sometimes even down to what illnesses we get. We don't just think our way into SMI, of course, but don't forget that people can make dramatic improvements in their daily functioning and quality of life just by changing their thought patterns. And so, we could also say that the mind achieves what it believes about itself.

Clearing harmful religious structures from my life in favor of a hope-filled Christianity healed me partially. The other essential change was ignoring books and scholarship describing my illness and what this meant about myself and my life trajectory. This was transformational.

Labels are permanent, and SMI is often, though by no means always, permanent. Research is not bad and reading scholarship is not bad, perhaps, so long as one takes it with a grain of salt. In general, I don't recommend it.

What makes SMI permanent? Not staying in treatment. Abusing drugs and alcohol. The first step is to acknowledge that you are greatly reducing your likelihood of a good life by being reckless and wishy-washy about treatment.

Assuming you're being careful, what else makes SMI permanent?

Reducing yourself to a label and seeing yourself as nothing more than a label and a set of symptoms that will always be there until you die.

SMI can last a lifetime, and in bad cases we probably need to stay on medicine, but we cannot leave it at that. As soon as we frame SMI as permanent, we're doomed to stagnate, or get worse!

As people, we read books or watch movies about life all the time. Eventually we can't tell if we are experiencing life the way we are because the book we've read changed us, or because the movie was so accurate that it captured us perfectly!

Diagnoses are like books about ourselves. Once we have them, it means we have found something that describes a part of us perfectly. But unfortunately, we then may let them define us completely. And our mind achieves what it believes about itself. The illness becomes permanent.

Once we have a mental health diagnosis and agree with it, then we know what we are to move away from. It is not that we have a container to hold us permanently. No! Instead think of it this way: we have a direction. A goal: lasting stability. Maybe even a full recovery! A diagnosis is a sign that we must do things that move us out of this symptom cluster. In other words, a motion away from our illness.

Above all, never give up hope that you will get better!

If you have a doctor who says you're only going to get worse, and who doesn't listen to you when you say you want to keep things positive, get a different doctor! Negativity is poison for your brain. Obviously if you're trying to get off of a mood-stabilizer (like Lithium or Lamictal) and you are bipolar, you probably shouldn't go off of it. I would not trust a doctor if they told me I did not need the medicine I take because I know that this is what keeps me high-functioning. But if a doctor paints an overarching doom and gloom picture, get a second opinion.

I will conclude with an example of my own experience:

I once had a doctor who said in my first visit that I was on a low dose of what I was on and that, even though I was doing great, I could expect to double it within the next year! And then continue to go up on it. This is a bad sign! Turns out she had been an emergency room doctor and was used to people in absolute crisis. It was her first year in private practice. She gave me the right medicine change, but I quickly got a different doctor.

I will always take my medicine and avoid stress and clear my calendar when it needs to happen, but we must find doctors who have realism—who don't just tell us to go off our meds—paired with hope and optimism. Labels and diagnoses frequently take away our ability to see that our suffering might not be permanent. And therefore, labels can make the mind achieve the doom that doctors tell us about and that we most fear.

i. How to Pray for Suffering People

About eight days after saying this, he climbed the mountain to pray, taking Peter, John, and James along. While he was in prayer, the appearance of his face changed and his clothes became blinding white. At once two men were there talking with him. They turned out to be Moses and Elijah—and what a glorious appearance they made!

—LUKE 9:28-31

WHEN I THINK BACK to how I felt in my late twenties, with career caving in, and marriage struggling, and a whole host of other problems I have not shared with anyone—an image comes into my mind. It is of my head, filled with sharp objects and utensils that cause pain when touched and when they touch each other. Stray objects jumbled in my mind that are exquisitely sensitive to my touch, professional intervention, and even prayer.

I don't know how I prayed for myself. I don't think I had the strength to do so. I can remember praying at the beginning of my illness—but I don't think I remembered to pray during the years when I was in the darkest part of it. And I don't blame myself for this. It is just how things were.

But I did ask others to pray on my behalf. And I believe that it helped a great deal.

Here's how I pray for people in absolute crisis and despair:

First, I imagine the person in their fullness and with their ailment, and see the ailment as a blockage of energy that is preventing them right now from seeing themselves as the child of God that they are and all that they are meant to be. It is painful to see the kink that is blocking them from their potential, and I remind myself how much stronger they will be for this ordeal once we get grace flowing through the system again. Once they're ready and able to ask for grace.

At first when I begin my prayer the person is my size—it's as though they are sitting right next to me. But then I shrink them down smaller into the size of the palm of my hand in my mind's eye . . . they become a little person in my palm, who is swollen with pain and suffering. I then imagine a golden ball of God's grace surrounding them and then around that I envision a bright white orb of protection and divine benevolence that will promote their healing.

The soul sufferer lies in this womb of golden grace and ethereal love, the love of Jesus, and I start imagining this grace and love surrounding the individual, watching as it permeates their skin, and then flows down into the lungs, and the heart, and the whole body and their entire being, and all the surrounding love of the room they are in. The glow is deep and warm because of the shocking love of it all, and I imagine this in my mind's eye.

I imagine their mind being made new in Christ and the hands of Jesus, with holes from the nails, cradling their head and massaging their temples and the holy space between the eyebrows as he brings them living water.

I pray that God would purify and cleanse the mind gradually, and thoroughly, and with care. I visualize this happening and the process by which they come to allow this to happen to themselves.

Prayers for people who are suffering in their soul need to be filled with hope. Imagine golden grace filling the top of the head and radiating throughout the body, clearing any blockages and erasing the shame that keeps the illness intact. Pray in a way that makes space for their future wellness.

j. When I Share . . .

*Now we look inside, and what we see is that anyone
united with the Messiah gets a fresh start, is created new.
The old life is gone; a new life emerges! Look at it!*

—2 CORINTHIANS 5:17

SOME PEOPLE, JUST BECAUSE they have been diagnosed with schizo-phrenia or bipolar disorder, kill themselves because of the stigma. They hate themselves for it and can't come to grips fast enough with a rapidly transformed self-image.

How did I avoid such a fate?

Even in my earliest period of intense struggle a diary entry shows I made the following commitment: that if I got through it, I was to help others like me. I learned this from AA. I had a friend in AA and in AA they talk about service. That as soon as we are out of the emergency mode, we should be focused on giving back to others in the earlier stages of recovery. People become greeters, sponsors, or help run the meetings. And it is beautiful.

How did I avoid such a fate?

I met with a pastor who assured me that SMI is not the devil.

How did I avoid such a fate?

Through another mentor I realized that God gives us doctors and medicine so that we can better meet his purposes and serve him in this life.

And I reminded myself that illness teaches us that we are not God. I am currently reading a book called *Blessed by Illness*. While

I think that that is taking it too far, and that it was probably written by someone who hadn't had a debilitating illness, I *do* think that people who are ill do well to try to learn something through their suffering.

I have noticed that it hurts to share my story with people who are not used to pain.

Or with people who are embarrassed by their pain and who feel that they are a lesser human for it.

When I share with people sometimes, the look I get back from them is pity. They do not realize that I'm proud of what I've been through, to have survived and to be able to share. And so even though it hurts to share when people feel like to understand me is to pity me, it heals me.

It heals me because I am a success story in a world where only the negative stories reach the news media and grape vine. And I am encouraged to weather their condescension until I find a listener who needs my words.

k. Fourteen Morning Questions to Start Your Day Right

I'll be with you as you do this, day after day after day, right up to the end of the age.

—MATTHEW 28:20

NO MATTER THE WAY we get up, *when* we get up . . . mornings can be a beautiful time to spend in silence, with a posture of listening and warmth.

Can you imagine feeling peace?

Gratitude?

Calm?

Maybe the sun is already shining when you awaken. Or maybe it is still dark. Either way, poets and mystics across the ages have cultivated sacred morning spaces to bridge the gap between sleep and wakefulness. It doesn't need to be every morning that you consider the following questions. But just try them out from time to time on difficult days when you need a mental detox or cleanse. Aren't sleeping well? Maybe they will be mid-morning questions . . .

1. Am I obsessing and despairing over a challenge that may be difficult but that I can deal with constructively after my morning routine?
2. Am I seeing someone as evil as if they could never redeem themselves? (Everyone is redeemable.)

3. Am I seeing something as a problem outside of myself when really it would be alleviated if I just thought about it from God's perspective? (Lay it at God's feet.)

4. In my insecurity, uncertainty, or defensiveness, am I seeing life as "me versus the world?" (Jesus has taken on the world and conquered via nonviolence.)

5. Am I thinking that a situation that was hurtful was directed at me, when really it is possible it had nothing to do with me? (Lean not on your own understanding.)

6. Am I over-generalizing, unable to see the good and where God is working in my life?

7. Am I angry or upset because of something going on now, that really is about something that happened in the past? Can I separate past from present? (See I am doing a new thing ...)

8. Am I taking in all aspects of a problem, or am I only seeing the bad in a situation that could be ambiguous? If someone else had been there, would they have come to the same conclusion? (Lean not on your own understanding.)

9. Have I been reading the New Testament (just the four Gospels, not anything else) to be in line with Jesus's wishes for my thought-life and actions during my days on earth?

10. Have I been listening with humility to voices from the margins that could put my suffering in perspective? (For example, books, podcasts, or articles by people of color, persons with disabilities, or other marginalized populations?)

11. Are my expectations and goals realistic? Sometimes what we are striving for isn't even based in the Bible about what God wants for our lives. Sometimes, if we have a disability, we think we should do one thing, when really, we are gifted for another.[1]

---

1. (Note, I know this one could seem super privileged, but sometimes people stay in a job that is making them suicidal/homicidal. If it's a matter of living or not, or of causing grave harm or not, then seriously reassess how you are spending your time and that your giftedness may have changed.)

12. Ask yourself: Do I really know what's going to happen in the future? Does anyone but God know what's in store? The answer is no. We are not God. We do not know.

13. Am I being a perfectionist? Am I being overly critical, forgetting that I am God's child?

14. Am I working in my areas of strength so I can live my life with confidence, joy and purpose?

1. Christian Contemplation

Peter said, "Change your life. Turn to God and be baptized,
each of you, in the name of Jesus Christ, so your sins are
forgiven. Receive the gift of the Holy Spirit. The promise is
targeted to you and your children, but also to all who are
far away—whomever, in fact, our Master God invites."

—ACTS 2:38-39

DOES BEING A CHRISTIAN change the way we are? Indeed, it should. Being a Christian should change the way we are. But what if we are incapacitated with SMI?

To strive means to hope, and psychosis is a state of disintegration. A sort of hope filters in, but this time it is the hope that comes from being aware that you are no longer striving. The hope that you will never defeat yourself or be defeated again because you are immobilized.

In a word, this is catatonia (which I have lived through).

Mindfulness meditation, based in Buddhism, perhaps saved my life, because I would make goals and then disintegrate from them and my life had become an exercise of building sandcastles . . . only to have the next hour's mood swing pulverize them. Through mindfulness, I acquired an added sense that I shouldn't have goals, which decreased my suicidality, but also put my life on hold and made me lose hope.

The principles of mindfulness still inform my life, but I have adapted them into the framework of Christianity, centering hope as a key feature. Take them with you as you go about your day.

NOT JUDGING:

"Don't pick on people, jump on their failures, criticize their faults—unless, of course, you want the same treatment. That critical spirit has a way of boomeranging. It's easy to see a smudge on your neighbor's face and be oblivious to the ugly sneer on your own. Do you have the nerve to say, 'Let me wash your face for you,' when your own face is distorted by contempt? It's this whole traveling road-show mentality all over again, playing a holier-than-thou part instead of just living your part. Wipe that ugly sneer off your own face, and you might be fit to offer a washcloth to your neighbor." (Matthew 7:2–5)

PATIENCE:

"Consider it a sheer gift, friends, when tests and challenges come at you from all sides. You know that under pressure, your faith-life is forced into the open and shows its true colors. So don't try to get out of anything prematurely. Let it do its work so you become mature and well-developed, not deficient in any way." (James 1:2–8)

BEING LIKE A CHILD, WITH A FRESH BEGINNING:

"For an answer Jesus called over a child, whom he stood in the middle of the room, and said, "I'm telling you, once and for all, that unless you return to square one and start over like children, you're not even going to get a look at the kingdom, let alone get in. Whoever becomes

56

simple and elemental again, like this child, will rank high in God's kingdom. What's more, when you receive the childlike on my account, it's the same as receiving me." (Matthew 18:2–5)

FAITH AND TRUST

"The fundamental fact of existence is that this trust in God, this faith, is the firm foundation under everything that makes life worth living. It's our handle on what we can't see. The act of faith is what distinguished our ancestors, set them above the crowd." (Hebrews 11: 1–2)

AVOIDING WORKS-RIGHTEOUSNESS— WE LIVE BY *GRACE* AND ARE SAVED BY *FAITH*—AND NOT OUR OWN EFFORTS

"Now God has us where he wants us, with all the time in this world and the next to shower grace and kindness upon us in Christ Jesus. Saving is all his idea, and all his work. All we do is trust him enough to let him do it. It's God's gift from start to finish! We don't play the major role. If we did, we'd probably go around bragging that we'd done the whole thing! No, we neither make nor save ourselves. God does both the making and saving. He creates each of us by Christ Jesus to join him in the work he does, the good work he has gotten ready for us to do, work we had better be doing." (Ephesians 2:7–10)

ACCEPTANCE AND SURRENDER

"He replied, 'You've been given insight into God's kingdom. You know how it works. Not everybody has this gift, this insight; it hasn't been given to them. Whenever someone has a ready heart for this, the insights and understandings flow freely. But if there is no readiness, any trace of receptivity soon disappears. That's why I tell stories: to create readiness, to nudge the people toward a welcome awakening. In their present state they can stare till doomsday and not see it, listen till they're blue in the face and not get it. I don't want Isaiah's forecast repeated all over again: Your ears are open but you don't hear a thing. Your eyes are awake but you don't see a thing. The people are stupid! They stick their fingers in their ears so they won't have to listen; They screw their eyes shut so they won't have to look, so they won't have to deal with me face-to-face and let me heal them.'" (Matthew 13:11–15)

HOPE

"God brings death and God brings life, brings down to the grave and raises up. God brings poverty and God brings wealth; he lowers, he also lifts up. He puts poor people on their feet again; he rekindles burned-out lives with fresh hope, Restoring dignity and respect to their lives— a place in the sun! For the very structures of earth are God's; he has laid out his operations on a firm foundation. He protectively cares for his faithful friends, step by step, but leaves the wicked to stumble in the dark. No one makes it in this life by sheer muscle! God's enemies will be blasted out of the sky, crashed in a heap and burned. God will set things right all over the earth, he'll give strength to his king, he'll set his anointed on top of the world!" (1 Samuel 2:6–10)

FORGIVENESS

"Seek God while he's here to be found, pray to him while he's close at hand. Let the wicked abandon their way of life and the evil their way of thinking. Let them come back to God, who is merciful, come back to our God, who is lavish with forgiveness." (Isaiah 55:6–7)

THANKSGIVING/PRAISE/WORSHIPFULNESS

"God appeared to Abram and said, 'I will give this land to your children.' Abram built an altar at the place God had appeared to him." (Genesis 12:7)

***

"Starting from the day you put the sickle to the ripe grain, count out seven weeks. Celebrate the Feast-of-Weeks to God, your God, by bringing your Freewill-Offering— give as generously as God, your God, has blessed you. Rejoice in the Presence of God, your God: you, your son, your daughter, your servant, your maid, the Levite who lives in your neighborhood, the foreigner, the orphan and widow among you; rejoice at the place God, your God, will set aside to be worshiped." (Deuteronomy 16:9–11)

***

"Celebrate God all day, every day. I mean, *revel* in him! Make it as clear as you can to all you meet that you're on their side, working with them and not against them. Help them see that the Master is about to arrive. He could show up any minute! Don't fret or worry. Instead of worrying, pray. Let petitions and praises shape your worries into prayers, letting God know your concerns. Before you know it, a sense of God's wholeness, everything coming together for good, will come and settle you down. It's wonderful what happens when Christ displaces worry at the center of your life." (Philippians 4:4–7)

***

"But the time is coming—it has, in fact, come—when what you're called will not matter and where you go to worship will not matter. 'It's who you are and the way you live that count before God. Your worship must engage your spirit in the pursuit of truth. That's the kind of people the Father is out looking for: those who are simply and honestly *themselves* before him in their worship. God is sheer being itself—Spirit. Those who worship him must do it out of their very being, their spirits, their true selves, in adoration.'" (John 4:21–24)

m. What the Schizophrenia Spectrum Teaches All of Us about Being Christian

In this way we are like the various parts of a human body.
Each part gets its meaning from the body as a whole,
not the other way around. The body we're talking about
is Christ's body of chosen people. Each of us finds our meaning
and function as a part of his body. But as a chopped-off finger
or cut-off toe we wouldn't amount to much, would we? So since
we find ourselves fashioned into all these excellently formed
and marvelously functioning parts in Christ's body, let's just
go ahead and be what we were made to be, without enviously
or pridefully comparing ourselves with each other, or trying
to be something we aren't. If you preach, just preach God's
Message, nothing else; if you help, just help, don't take over;
if you teach, stick to your teaching; if you give encouraging
guidance, be careful that you don't get bossy; if you're put in
charge, don't manipulate; if you're called to give aid to people
in distress, keep your eyes open and be quick to respond; if you
work with the disadvantaged, don't let yourself get irritated
with them or depressed by them. Keep a smile on your face.

—ROMANS 12:4–8

MANY CHRISTIANS WORRY ABOUT the varieties of Christianity that are emerging all over the globe—Christians often declare opposing Christianities "un-Christian." And this is to our detriment and to the detriment of would-be fellow believers seeking Christ in a crisis. In this essay I talk about how my unique worldview as a sufferer of schizoaffective disorder has allowed me to see the typically warring sides of Christianity with compassion. I advocate for an unconventional approach to our political and spiritual differences by drawing on a story from my husband Todd's and my life.

SO MANY CHURCHES, SO MANY VALUES

One church believes x, the other believes y. Which one is right? Meanwhile, I'm suffering! I need a pastor! Where do I go if I'm gay? Where do I go if I'm having an affair? Where do I go if I'm being abused? The questions abound . . . and having worshiped at multiple churches with radically different perspectives on all of these topics regularly several days a week for the past several years, I can tell you that churches can have radically different answers to these questions . . . and generally they will think that they are the only one offering the right answer.

One church would never allow divorce, even in the face of the gravest abuse, while the other will marry gay couple or happily advise a divorce in the face of "mere" irreconcilable differences. One church cares about social justice, and the other cares about building a personal relationship with Jesus as their Savior. My favorite book ever is by Douglas Strong at Seattle Pacific University on how people can be Evangelical and invested in social justice at the same time. It is a little old, but it provides examples of people who have done this. You should read it.

Meanwhile, a hurting individual has just walked into a church, *your* church. What do we do? They don't know anything about Christianity. They read a blog (like this one) that suggested they give it a try . . .

WHERE'S THE COMPASSION? A TRICK QUESTION

I'm going to draw a parallel that will shed further light on the situation. I'm reminded of a recent conversation that I had with my husband Todd about what we would do when the time came for our dog, Addie (age ten), to be put down. Now I'll preface this by saying that if you are reading this in a country other than the US, feel free to laugh at this example—Americans are ridiculous about their dogs; they are our children. Anyway, Todd had just read a recent article in the *New York Times* about hospice for dogs. He earnestly texted me the link during the day and then brought it up at dinner expectantly that night, seeking my blessing that when our girl gets near the end, we would do hospice.

I, on the other hand, thought that that would be completely unnecessary. But I knew it was important to him and was determined not to belittle the tender idea that was beginning to take hold. I said that I would support hospice up until I thought it would be unethical to keep her alive. At which point I would leave town to leave him with Addie since I wouldn't dream of putting her down before Todd was ready.

This seemed like the perfect American boundaries, just like what I had studied as a psychology student. It was even allowing my dear girl to suffer longer just to please my husband. What a sacrifice on my part! Can you imagine the anguish . . . ?

The impact of this comment, however, was unexpected.

"So then you would leave me to shoulder the loss all by myself?" Todd asked, crestfallen. "How could you do such a thing? Where's the compassion?"

I couldn't hold back my frustration at this unexpected turn. You see I was thinking that I had already thrown Todd a bone— forgive the expression—by even saying hospice would be okay. And now even by honoring traditional boundaries and deciding to remove myself from the situation to honor Todd's feelings, I was wrong.

"How would I be uncompassionate"—which isn't a word, by the way—"by leaving you with her so she could die the way you wanted?" I told Todd. "You'd be winning! Why would you lack compassion and prolong her suffering in the first place?"

Addie was sitting there, meanwhile, in perfect health, watching the argument take off.

"You think that putting her down is compassionate?" Todd said. "Americans only put down their animals to make their lives easier!"

WHICH CHURCH IS MODELING CHRIST?

The ultimate question was what compassion looked like, but we didn't frame it that way. It was more personal: it was which of us was compassionate. It could not be both. The parallels with the state of American Christianity may already be clear to those who remember that the litmus test of any Christianity is this: are we modeling Christ? Modeling Christ is the top value. And what it looks like is different for each side.

Broken church, we must ask ourselves if we are looking beyond ourselves and seeking the mind of Christ—and yet, already a new argument arises. Whose version of the mind of Christ is the right version? Round and round we go . . .

I have learned that focusing on our own healing or the possibility of a cure for ourselves is not how we heal ourselves. It is also not how we heal the world. Stop asking how the church can heal. It can't. It's a part of the fallen creation. The more we try to convert everyone to our side, the more contentious matters will become and the church will fracture as permanently as when the veil of the temple was torn in two.

Part of being on the schizophrenia spectrum—when it's untreated, mine is treated—means that you're living in multiple realities at once. I have been able to immerse myself in different worldviews entirely, while others do this merely as a thought experiment with a charitable perspective of "humoring" the opposition before invalidating them. I can really occupy multiple worldviews, fully and at once.

I have learned that God works through us even when we're at our most broken when we look outside of ourselves. At my lowest point I asked God, as Jesus did, "Why have you forsaken me?" This is an act of utter humility. Maybe that's what we need to do before the church finds new life, to die to ourselves and to our egos which are ripping it apart to the detriment of those who need to be healed.

AN UNCONVENTIONAL SOLUTION

We must each follow the Holy Spirit's call to what our church, or our institution is meant to be. As Christians of a broken twenty-first-century Christianity the trap lies in our trying to be everything to everyone. Let some churches be conservative. Let some be liberal. Try to persuade others to your side. But don't dehumanize people or dismiss them and their Christianity as if that makes them unworthy of Christ's kingdom. Don't say someone is oppressing you just because they have a different worldview. People should be allowed to have differing callings. Who even knows what those labels mean in the first place? They mean a different thing to every person.

Afterword

Schools and Mental Health

Point your kids in the right direction—
when they're old they won't be lost.

—PROVERBS 22:6

THERE IS SOMETHING AMISS in schools nowadays: they aren't helping people to learn and grow with tentativeness and humility. We have made teachers into gods and they disciple our children without an integrated Christian worldview. And those in the church can also be lacking in a Christian worldview. It's not integrated. It's not holistic.

Often, in schools, people lack humility. We lack humility if we are fundamentalist for the same reason that we lack humility if we are liberals, or that we lack humility as conservatives: it is exceptionalism-based thinking. We think there is only one right answer and that it is, coincidentally—imagine that—*ours*! When we try to reconcile science and religion as liberals and Evangelicals, we are doing what quantum physics attempted to do as well. Pauli with psychoanalysis and archetypes and Qabalah; Bohr with the Tao and Chinese philosophy; Schrödinger with Hindu philosophy; Heisenberg with the Platonic theory of ancient Greece.

I would argue that the Wesleyan concept of combining knowledge with vital piety addressed a need during his time (the eighteenth century) that continues to this day. It is something that we would do well to remember, given the Wesleyan strain still prevalent in American thought. The idea of political correctness, itself, is a sort of social sanctification whereby holiness is attained through words. I completely get why some people sneer at political correctness for the sake of political correctness. Deprived of the religious undertones, it can lead to the exceptionalism I have been describing. But political correctness, when thoughtfully used, is a sign of respect and is no longer political.

Let me put it this way: we forget, when outside of the Christian frame (but still striving for perfection) that we are not God. To say what is right or "politically correct," is not always to think what is right and believe what is right. And therefore, it is not right action. Though it's not bigotry, it won't be sustainable. There is not alignment with what in theology we talk about as the "horizontal" and the "vertical" aspects of existence. There is not alignment, in other words, with "community" and "submission" to something more powerful than us. In other words, to God. What does "perfect" speech, in other words, politically correct speech, point to without God? How can we be sure that we are acting in Christian charity and love? Religion is what teaches us such alignment. And secularism will never get there. But neither will fundamentalism, for the very same reason.

John Wesley, the founder of what later came to be the Methodist strain of Christianity, dealt with the science and religion debate as well as with political and religious in-fighting in a sermon called "The Catholic Spirit" that finds its embodiment today in Wesleyan schools. While they're not perfect, and are currently embroiled in conflict around human sexuality, what they are *trying* to do is a start. Wesleyan Christian education is precisely what is needed in the US. It is not esoteric. It mixes knowledge and vital piety, and also social action. Social engagement, not reclusiveness. Schools that disciple students, and that unite piety and knowledge in a way that destabilizes the dominance of whiteness in higher education today, over time could allow us as a culture to mature past our liberal and conservative, scientific and religious, fundamentalisms. I firmly believe that some of the mental health crisis would be avoided if we could inculcate faith into the curricula. We are designed to be faithful, and we are believing creatures.

My Daily Go-To's

My dear friends, don't believe everything you hear.
Carefully weigh and examine what people tell you.
Not everyone who talks about God comes from God.
There are a lot of lying preachers loose in the world.

—1 JOHN 4:1

DON'T FORGET THAT I am neither clergy, a theologian, nor a mental health therapist/psychiatrist. *Never prioritize what I say here above the advice of professionals, medical or spiritual.*

- I recommend the devotional portions of Dr. Peter J. Bellini's *Truth Therapy* if you are looking for a holistic lens to healing body, mind, and soul that gets into the mind in particular, and immerses us in Scripture. Start in the middle chapters, specifically chapters 4 and 5, since the first chapters are for experts. Chapter 5 I use as a devotional daily.[2] I have met Dr. Bellini and felt the anointing of the Holy Spirit in his presence. He is a godly man and he really cares.

- Be selective of what mental health memoirs you read. There is, admittedly, something healing about reading books by people who are living well with their condition; however, a lot of them push people into an immoral lifestyle. Exercise discernment.

2. Bellini, *Truth Therapy*, 68–253.

- The two secular memoirs I recommend are *The Center Cannot Hold*, by Dr. Elyn Saks, and *An Unquiet Mind*, by Dr. Kay Redfield Jamison. Both were instrumental in getting me to see how common it was for me to be triggered and to blame the trigger on the actual event rather than the fact that my brain was ill-equipped to deal with any stress.

- The Christian memoir I recommend is *Darkness Is My Only Companion*, by Kathryn Greene-McCreight. Unlike me, she is ordained. She suffers from bipolar disorder and is a theologian with a PhD. As the title suggests, she experiences her illness as darkness. I don't experience mine that way. It's important to remember that if you do, you're not alone. Her book will help you find meaning.

- Be selective of what books about SMI you read. If you yourself are struggling with psychosis, avoid books like *Insane Consequences*, by D. J. Jaffe, which pathologize people with SMI and lump us all into one basket—namely, the criminal basket—and also diminish our ability to trust our doctors. I have schizoaffective disorder, and a few people who have had it have caused great harm. Reading about this gets me down a dark rabbit hole meditating on the ungodly things people have done while ill with my diagnosis. Don't focus on that, and have confidence in the medical care you receive, wherever possible.

- If you are worried you are missing out by not reading everything on the topic of mental health, have loved ones read the books that are negative. Jaffe, for example, has devoted his life to supporting people with SMI and is to be commended; however, his book opens with mug shots of mentally ill criminals. It is not therapeutic or uplifting to read, and there are many books like this out there that I wish I had avoided from the beginning.

- Meditate on what is holy and focus on how you can continue to serve God's human community, even if it's just by praying—continue to take your medicine and have faith that you will find stability. Don't read disturbing books, or study bad things people have done.

- If you are caring for someone who is experiencing mental health challenges or are a church member supporting someone with SMI, read *Troubled Minds*, by Amy Simpson.

- If you are a pastor or other professional who encounters Christian sufferers of SMI who have experienced trauma, including sexual trauma from Christian leaders, read *The Back Side of the Cross* by Rev. Drs. Brent Peterson and Diane Leclerc. The book is steeped in consciousness of the special burdens to healing the church itself sometimes places on victims of violence, abandonment, sexual, and other forms of abuse. For example, some pastors will urge forgiveness without qualifying what that should look like given the perhaps devastating trauma that has occurred, or victims will be urged to stay quiet to keep the peace or to protect the image of a leader. The authors demonstrate that too often in the local church the focus is on sinners and not the sinned-against, and they provide robust supports for being Christ not only to sinners but to the sinned-against.

- As a church, you should have a safety plan so you are prepared for danger—don't be ignorant or unprepared. But nurture the goodness of the person and focus on Amy Simpson's work. Most persons with SMI won't hurt you. We are much more likely to hurt ourselves or to be the victims of crime. Furthermore, we are sensitive when perceived as a threat; it only makes our lives harder.

- For a comprehensive worldview of what I propose, written by a pastor and professor of theology and disability, and a doctor of nursing practice, read *Christian Ethics and Nursing Practice*, by Drs. Richard B. Steele and Heidi A. Monroe. The book integrates the four strands of biblical moral discourse (law, holiness, wisdom and prophecy) with the American Nursing Code. I have read the book at least five times because I know Dr. Steele and that he walks the talk (my correspondence with him ends my book).

- If a person expresses intent to harm others or self, take it seriously and seek professional help or call 911.

Emergency Resources and Hotlines

Don't be afraid, I've redeemed you.
I've called your name. You're mine.
When you're in over your head, I'll be there with you.
When you're in rough waters, you will not go down.
When you're between a rock and a hard place,
it won't be a dead end—

—ISAIAH 43:2

- *911—this is for immediate danger. Tell the operator that a person is experiencing a psychiatric emergency, and advocate that police officers come with a crisis counselor or that they send police with this training.*

- *988 Suicide and Crisis Lifeline—If you dial or text 988 you can access a crisis counselor 24/7. I used this number before my hospitalizations and it really, really helped. They were non-judgmental and heard me as I shared about my thoughts. They also connect you to supports in your local setting.*

- *NAMI Crisis Text line—Text NAMI to 741-741*

- *National Domestic Violence Hotline—800-799-SAFE (7233)—They will give confidential support and give you further information on how to get help/resources.*

- *National Sexual Assault Hotline—800-656-HOPE (4673)—Free help 24/7 that connects you with trained staff.*

Bibliography

Bellini, Peter J. *Truth Therapy: Renewing Your Mind with the Word of God.* Eugene, OR: Wipf & Stock, 2014.

Greene-McCreight, Kathryn. *Darkness Is My Only Companion: A Christian Response to Mental Illness.* Grand Rapids, MI: Brazos, 2006.

Jamison, Kay Redfield. *An Unquiet Mind: A Memoir of Moods and Madness.* New York: Vintage, 1996.

Kristoff, Nicholas D., and Sheryl WuDunn. *Tightrope: Americans Reaching for Hope.* New York: Penguin Random House, 2020.

Leclerc, Diane. *Discovering Christian Holiness: The Heart of Wesleyan-Holiness Theology.* Kansas City, MO: Beacon Hill, 2010.

Leclerc, Diane, and Brent Peterson. *The Back Side of the Cross: An Atonement Theology for the Abused and Abandoned.* Eugene, OR: Cascade, 2022.

Levine, Peter A. *In an Unspoken Voice: How the Body Releases Trauma and Restores Goodness.* Berkeley, CA: North Atlantic, 2010.

Menakem, Resmaa. *My Grandmother's Hands: Racialized Trauma and the Pathway to Mending Our Hearts and Bodies.* Las Vegas: Central Recovery, 2017.

Rothstein, Richard. *The Color of Law: A Forgotten History of How Our Government Segregated America.* New York: Liveright, 2017.

Saks, Elyn. *The Center Cannot Hold: My Journey through Madness.* New York: Hyperion, 2007.

Salter McNeil, Brenda. *Becoming Brave: Finding the Courage to Pursue Racial Justice Now.* Grand Rapids, MI: Brazos, 2020.

———. *A Credible Witness: Reflections on Power Evangelism and Race.* Downers Grove, IL: InterVarsity, 2008.

Simpson, Amy. *Troubled Minds: Mental Illness and the Church's Mission.* Westmont, IL: InterVarsity, 2013.

Steele, Richard B., and Heidi A. Monroe. *Christian Ethics and Nursing Practice.* Eugene, OR: Cascade, 2020.

Strong, Douglas M. *They Walked in the Spirit: Personal Faith and Social Action in America.* Louisville, KY: Westminster John Knox, 1997.

BIBLIOGRAPHY

Vance, J. D. *Hillbilly Elegy: A Memoir of a Family and Culture in Crisis.* New York: HarperCollins, 2016.

Zimbardo, Philip, et al. *The Time Cure: Overcoming PTSD with the New Psychology of Time Perspective Therapy.* San Francisco: Jossey-Bass, 2012.

Index

INDEX

1. *The majority of the appendix features blog posts.*